# Romantic Responses to Revolution through Miltonic Ideas of the Fall

*Romantic Responses to Revolution through Miltonic Ideas of the Fall* explores the influence of John Milton's epic poem, *Paradise Lost*, on a range of Romantic and post-Romantic writers. Specifically, the book examines the way in which these writers use the Fall, and the notion of 'fallenness'—as envisioned in *Paradise Lost*—as a model for writing about their roles as poets/writers in periods of political and cultural turmoil.

This book will be of value to undergraduate and postgraduate students of English Literature with a specific interest in the Romantics. The writers and texts featured—including the 'big six' of Romantic poets, and three canonical novels of the early nineteenth century—are very widely studied on English Literature courses across the UK, US, and Europe. This makes the book an ideal reference text or inspiration point for essays, coursework, and theses, while the concise and accessible style should be especially appealing for undergraduates and lecturers looking for an approachable overview of Romantic responses to revolution and the influence of Milton.

**Callum Fraser** currently works as a commissioning editor at CRC Press/Taylor & Francis. He received a PhD from Newcastle University in 2018 for research on the influence of Milton on the Romantics, as well as a related creative project. He maintains his interest in this literary period and is currently working on a Gothic novel set in rural Cumberland in 1824.

# Routledge Focus on Literature

**Reading Modernity, Modernism and Religion Today**
Spinoza and Van Gogh
*Patrick Grant*

**The Sagas of Icelanders**
An Introduction to All Forty Sagas with Summaries
*Annette Lassen*

**Pandemics and Apocalypse in World Literature**
The Hope for Planetary Salvation
*William Franke*

**Reading Kazuo Ishiguro's *Never Let Me Go***
The Alternative Dystopian Imagination
*Eva Pelayo Sañudo*

**Romantic Responses to Revolution through Miltonic Ideas of the Fall**
*Callum Fraser*

For more information about this series, please visit: www.routledge.com/Routledge-Focus-on-Literature/book-series/RFLT

# Romantic Responses to Revolution through Miltonic Ideas of the Fall

**Callum Fraser**

NEW YORK AND LONDON

First published 2025
by Routledge
605 Third Avenue, New York, NY 10158

and by Routledge
4 Park Square, Milton Park, Abingdon, Oxon, OX14 4RN

*Routledge is an imprint of the Taylor & Francis Group, an informa business*



ISBN: 9781032864228 (hbk)
ISBN: 9781032864334 (pbk)
ISBN: 9781003527466 (ebk)

DOI: 10.4324/9781003527466

Typeset in Times New Roman
by Deanta Global Publishing Services, Chennai, India

# Contents

# Preface

The genesis of this book, if I can begin with a Miltonic pun, was a PhD which I began in 2014. The nature of the PhD called for a long-form creative piece (in my case a novel), and an accompanying critical thesis that spoke to the craft and themes of the creative work. Unlike most of my peers, I took a slightly back-to-front approach to this task by first writing the critical thesis and then the novel. Instead of using the critical piece as a vehicle to interrogate my own words, I took the opportunity to indulge in a piece of academic research on a topic that interested me—Milton and the Romantics—and to use this as inspirational fodder for the creative work.

I won't bore you with details of the novel itself, save to say that it remains a work-in-progress. What I think is important for readers of *this* book to take away from the story of its beginnings is how it shapes the approach the book takes to its subject: that I was engaged in an act of critical reading that formed the basis of a creative response. This is the basic principle that underlies this book's thesis: that literary efforts do not come into being ex nihilo, but are instead a reaction to the world framed by our reading of others.

In *Poetry and Repression* (1976), Harold Bloom wrote that 'Any poem is an inter-poem, and any reading of that poem is an inter-reading. A poem is not writing, but re-writing'.[1] Bloom's wider theories on poetic heredity are by no means universally accepted and are often regarded as too opaque and theoretically impenetrable for modern tastes. David Frite, in the preface to *Harold Bloom: The Rhetoric of Romantic Vision* (1985), makes the devastatingly dry remark that his book can serve as 'a clearly enough written' and 'less painful substitute for the "experience" of Bloom himself'.[2]

However, Bloom's essential point, shorn of self-obscuring abstractions, provides the template for this book. At its heart, it is concerned with how writers articulate their responses to the world through their reading and 're-writing' of their literary peers and forerunners.

In writing this book, I have selected the writers who best suit the purpose of my argument. Bloom would no doubt have approved of most of the choices, since he regarded Milton and the 'big six' Romantic poets—five of whom I address directly, with Percy Shelley also featuring—as 'strong' poets. In Bloom's words:

> Poetic history [...] is held to be indistinguishable from poetic influence, since strong poets make that history by misreading one another, so as to clear imaginative space for themselves.[3]

Bloom makes much of this idea of 'misreading', and one should look to *The Anxiety of Influence* (1973) and *A Map of Misreading* (1975) for more on this. In my own view, however, if the writers under discussion here do misread one another it is typically with a deliberate purpose.

Yes, one could argue they may miscast the intentions of other writers as a means to 'clear space' for their own efforts to be viewed as more original than they might otherwise appear. However, in the main I see nothing so petty as this, but rather a shared sensibility which spans generations and invites interaction. The Romantic and post-Romantic texts that this book deals with are not mere re-writings based upon false readings of *Paradise Lost* (1667). They are instead texts which borrow the structures, themes, and *ideas* of that poem in a bid to craft literature as new and original as the events to which they respond.

And indeed, it is the historical perspective which binds me to these particular writers, as opposed to Bloom's grandiose notions of 'strength'. Both the poets and the novelists discussed here are bound to *Paradise Lost* in particular because each is writing in response to a climate of post-revolutionary malaise, and such work can find no grander model than Milton's epic, and no more apt a hero for processing their despond than Satan, or rather Milton *through* Satan. As Bloom himself has it:

> The motto to English poetry since Milton was stated by Keats: 'Life to him would be Death to me.' This deathly vitality in Milton is the state of Satan in him, and is shown us not so much by the character of Satan in *Paradise Lost* as by Milton's editorializing relationship to his own Satan, and by his relationship to all the stronger poets of the eighteenth century and to most of those in the nineteenth.[4]

What Bloom gestures towards here is that *Paradise Lost* is not only a poem that concerns the greatest revolution of them all—that against God himself—but it is also a poem about poetry and poets. It treats poetry and literature as a tool with which to respond to revolution, as well as an instrument of revolution in itself, and provides a model for future poets to explore this function. Each of the writers I discuss in this book has a need of this model, whether it is the Romantic poets responding to the failure of the French Revolution to realise a political ideal, or the Romantic and post-Romantic novelists struggling to interpret the transition from one literary, political, and societal epoch to the next.

History—literary or otherwise—may rhyme, but it seldom repeats itself.

## Notes

1 Harold Bloom, *Poetry and Repression* (New Haven: Yale University Press, 1976), p. 3.
2 David Fite, *Harold Bloom: The Rhetoric of Romantic Vision* (Amherst: Amherst University Press, 1985), p. xi.
3 Harold Bloom, *The Anxiety of Influence* (Oxford: Oxford University Press, 1997), p. 5.
4 Harold Bloom, *The Anxiety of Influence* (Oxford: Oxford University Press, 1997), p. 32.

# Acknowledgements

I would like to give particular thanks to my wife, Catherine, and to my parents, Hamish and Jane. Without their support I would never have been in a position to write this book. I must also express my gratitude to Dr. Meiko O'Halloran and Dr. Margaret Wilkinson, who helped me immeasurably during the PhD which formed the basis of this work. I hope they will see this book as a worthy product of their kindness and guidance. Finally, thank you to Michelle Salyga and Bryony Reece for their editorial assistance, as well as the production team at Routledge for all of their help in making this book a reality.

# Introduction

This book is divided into two parts. The first part concerns five of the most significant Romantic poets: William Blake, Samuel Taylor Coleridge, William Wordsworth, Lord Byron and John Keats, while the second examines what we might term Romantic and post-Romantic novelists: James Hogg, Mary Shelley, and Emily Brontë. Throughout the book, I will explore how each of these writers uses Miltonic ideas of the Fall in their responses to the turbulent political and artistic periods in which they were writing.

It is of course well established that John Milton, and *Paradise Lost* in particular, had an immense influence on the Romantics. Lucy Newlyn even credits the poem with providing a template for poetic 'sublimity' in the Romantic period.[1] But in this book I wish to offer a particular focus on the way in which these writers use Miltonic ideas of the Fall to define their own role in responding to revolutions, whether political, literary, or societal.

But what are 'Miltonic ideas of the Fall', and why should they bear any particular significance to a group of people writing more than a century after Milton's death? To understand, we must first turn to Milton's most famous work, *Paradise Lost*:

> Full of doubt I stand,
> Whether I should repent me now of sin
> By me done and occasioned, or rejoice
> Much more that much more good thereof shall spring[2]

These lines, spoken by Adam in the final book of *Paradise Lost*, describe one of the central ideas of the Miltonic Fall. In essence, it is a contradiction: the Original Sin, the taking of knowledge, is a *necessary* fall. It equips mankind with the tools to understand their own evil, but also the potential to achieve Grace, evoking a clash between Jesuit pragmatism and Puritan idealism. William Blake famously confronted this tension when he wrote that:

> the reason Milton wrote in fetters when he wrote
> of Angels and God, and at liberty when of Devils and Hell

DOI: 10.4324/9781003527466-1

> is because he was a true poet, and of the Devil's party
> Without knowing it[3]

In my opinion, Milton may have been more cognisant of the link than Blake gave him credit for. In his book, *Milton and the Idea of the Fall* (2005), William Poole describes a 'dynamic, potentially dangerous Milton'—in my view a 'fallen' Milton—who subverts the traditional notions of his political, religious, and poetical orthodoxy in order to uphold a greater good.[4]

This is why I prefer the term 'necessary' fall over the more commonly used 'fortunate' fall, or 'felix culpa'. Arthur O. Lovejoy grapples with this definitional question in his influential essay 'Milton and the Paradox of the Fortunate Fall' (1937). I tend to agree with the reading that posits the Fall was 'not only a "happy fault"'—a reading that I think would be implied by use of the word 'fortunate'—but rather '"certainly necessary"—necessary to the very possibility of the redemptive act'.[5]

I would like to build upon this idea of the Fall, and fallenness more generally, as being necessary with a specific focus on *Paradise Lost*, and argue that the poem introduces deliberate and marked parallels between Milton and the fallen angel, Satan. In particular, I will suggest that Satan is a 'fallen' poet figure within the text, and that this manner of fallenness, as framed by *Paradise Lost*, shapes the manner in which the Romantics subsequently craft their literary responses to revolution.

To understand what is meant by a 'fallen' poet figure—and why that fallenness is so necessary—it is first important to be clear about what I mean by the term 'poet figure'. In the words of Daniel Morse, these are characters which inhabit the text of a poem, providing a 'reflective and contemplative' avatar for the poet.[6] For many scholars, this is the role of the epic narrator in *Paradise Lost.* His opening assertion that he will 'justify the ways of God to Men' (*PL*, 1. 26) has led some to suggest that Milton is directly assuming the role of 'mediator between God and man'. Indeed, Michael Leib suggests that he assumes a role of 'prophet, king and priest'; a triumvirate which characterises the poet figure as one who is privy to both the spiritual and the temporal spheres, and one who is bound to share this knowledge.[7]

The idea that the narrator is there to represent Milton has been used to dismiss the idea of a sympathetic link with Satan. Frank Kermode, in 'Adam Unparadised' (1960), asserts the 'epic poet's privilege of intervening in his own voice'.[8] For Kermode, the epic voice is there to provide a direct interpretation of the poem from Milton himself. For instance, during the demonic council, where Satan and his fellow Fallen Angels are at the height of their persuasive oratories, the epic narrator injects a note of caution:

> By falsities and lies the greatest part
> Of mankind they corrupted to forsake

> God their Creator, and th' invisible
> Glory of him that made them transform
> Oft to the image of a brute, adorned
> With gay religions full of pomp and gold,
> And devils to adore for deities
>
> (*PL*, 1. 367–373)

This Puritanical attack on the sinfulness of decorative religious expression appears to be a direct reflection of Milton's personal views, and it makes a compelling case for Kermode's argument.

However, more recent critics, such as Peter Herman, have observed that 'the speeches of the fallen angels recycle elements of Milton's own prose'.[9] For example, in *The Readie and Easie Way* (1660), an anti-monarchist tract written seven years before the first publication of *Paradise Lost*, Milton pours scorn on Charles I and his courtiers, writing of how he would 'pageant himself up and down in progress among the perpetual bowings and scrapings of an abject people, on either side deifying and adoring him'.[10] In a reflection of this, Satan rhetorically inquires of his fellow demons, still recumbent after their defeat, 'in this abject posture have ye sworn/ To adore the Conqueror?' (*PL*, 1. 322–323). The similarity of Satan's 'political' rhetoric to Milton's would seem to disrupt Kermode's assertion that the epic narrator is the sole mouthpiece of the poet.

If we return to the three roles of the poet figure which Leib identifies: prophet, king, and priest, the issue becomes further complicated. It is Satan who introduces the 'ancient and prophetic' (*PL*, 2. 346) rumours of Earth, and it is he who sits on the 'throne of royal state' (*PL*, 2. 1). And yet, the epic narrator could be deemed the priestlier of the two, as it is he who invokes the names of saints, and of God himself, throughout the poem. What we have, it seems, is a splitting of the poet figure. Catherine Bates describes Satan as fashioning 'himself poetically [...] from one self-authored role, or "borrowed visage" to another'.[11] But this argument does not go far enough. The epic narrator and Satan are themselves borrowed visages—each a different mask for Milton, each a different aspect of the poet figure.

What is happening here is a reassertion of the poem's central conflict between good and evil. In his polemic on the freedom of the press, *The Areopagitica* (1644), Milton describes the awkward relationship between these moral opposites:

> Good and evil we know in the field of this world grow up together almost inseparably; and the knowledge of good is so involved and interwoven with the knowledge of evil, and in so many cunning resemblances hardly to be discerned [...] It was from out of the rind of one apple tasted that the knowledge of good and evil, as two twins cleaving together, leaped forth into the world.[12]

Just as the apple contains knowledge of both good and evil, so too does the poet figure. What the poem has done is to separate these two binary strands, and to give each a face. Satan is evil—it is he who tempts Eve into knowledge. The narrator is good—he seeks to direct that knowledge toward the good and to justify the ways of God.

*Paradise Lost*, then, can begin to be seen as something more than just an epic about morality, but about the specific morality of poets and poetry. Sigmund Freud's description of the poet is of a child at play, always seeking to 'rearrange the things of his world in a way which pleases him'.[13] And of course, this is what Milton has done with *Paradise Lost*, taking the Bible and reimagining its content. It is a curiously subversive act for a man so famously Puritan. Poole makes the point that there are those even today who consider 'such literary attempts to be impious, shaking the walls of the world [by] talking about things using the wrong language'.[14] And yet, Milton clearly believes that this potential irreverence is justified. In Book Five, the angel Raphael neatly summarises the concept. Forced to relate the events of the conflict in Heaven to Adam and Eve, he asks:

> how shall I relate [...]
> The secrets of another world, perhaps
> Not lawful to reveal? Yet for thy good
> This is dispensed.
>
> (*PL*, 5. 564–570)

This is the very essence of the conflict between the two sides of the poet figure. On the one hand is the motive to achieve something good—the enlightenment of mankind. On the other is the necessity of sin to achieve it. In *Paradise Lost*, the poet figure has been physically divided. The narrator is all motive—the virtuous desire, like Raphael, to impart knowledge of a higher realm—but it is Satan who achieves the desired ends through the temptation of Eve.

Of course, one might suggest that this reading of the poem undermines Milton's primary purpose. He is, after all, making a broad point about the relationship between God and humanity in general. To suggest this is an allegory specifically about poets would seem a private conceit rather than an act of virtue. Milton himself warns us of the dangers of allegory and metaphor in his philosophical treatise, *The Art of Logic* (1672), published after *Paradise Lost*:

> warning [...] should be given that likes whether of short or full form are not to be urged beyond that quality which the man making the comparison intended to show as the same in both [...] Nothing similar is identical; likeness does not run four feet; every likeness hobbles.[15]

And yet, if we focus on the character of Satan, the temptation is to deepen the allegory still further. If we return to Freud's understanding of the poet, as one who does not so much create, but rearranges the world around them, we find that Satan does exactly the same thing. In Book One he observes that the 'mind is its own place, and in itself/ Can make a Heaven of Hell, a Hell of Heaven' (*PL*, 1. 254–255). He seems to be signposting his role in this allegory as the creative force of the poet. This position is reinforced by Satan's relationship with Chaos: the thing which separates Heaven and Hell from Earth. This barrier is described by the narrator as a realm of:

> Rumour [...] Chance
> And Tumult, and Confusion, all embroiled,
> And Discord with a thousand various mouths
>
> (*PL*, 2. 965–967)

Here, Satan is faced with a malleable, disordered world that he must make sense of. Indeed, he does not merely need to impose an order on it, but to make a bridge of it—a physical thing to connect together the spiritual and temporal spheres. The 'broad and beaten way' that Satan creates 'Over the dark abyss' (*PL*, 2. 1026–1027) can be seen as an allegory of poetic construction itself. It is a physical realisation of creative thought.

But if *Paradise Lost* is, in part, a self-reflexive piece about the nature of poets and poetry, does this give credence to the view that this is an inward-looking work, more about Milton's own personal relationship with God than with humanity as a whole? Again, we are forced to turn to the epic narrator, and to consider the duality of the poet figure. The narrator appears acutely conscious of the risk that *Paradise Lost* might be perceived as an exercise in egotism, and at the very beginning of the poem seeks to negate this. Addressing the Muse, the narrator implores: 'O Spirit [...] Instruct me, for Thou know'st' (*PL*, 1. 17–19). He deliberately debases his own attributes and seeks to attribute any greater skill or wisdom onto the Muse itself: 'what in me is dark/ Illumine, what is low raise and support' (*PL*, 1. 22–23). Any hint of arrogance is pushed firmly onto Satan.

We see this action repeated throughout the poem. In the scene following her creation, Eve comes close to an act of egotism:

> As I bent down to look, just opposite,
> A shape within the wat'ry gleam appeared,
> Bending to look on me. I started back
> It started back; but pleased I soon returned.
>
> (*PL*, 4. 460–461)

She does not complete this narcissistic act of self-love, however, as she is joined by Adam, to whom her affection is turned instead. Her conduct here is 'a fall averted', a fact which Milton signposts before the event.[16] Indeed, it is God himself who proclaims that Satan's Fall is 'self-tempted, self depraved', whereas Eve 'falls, deceived/ By the other' (*PL*, 3. 130–131).

What we see here is the re-emergence of a pattern within the poem of Satan being used as a device to offset the sin of others; a pattern that can only endorse the view of him as a poet figure. Satan's crime is the same as Narcissus: he esteems himself above others. And yet it is this flaw in his character that drives him to tempt mankind into knowledge of good and evil. His sin provides humanity with the eventual key to salvation. This, then, is the gift of Milton and Satan. Milton's own God predicts that humanity will 'find grace' (*PL*, 3. 131) through knowledge of their own sin. Thus, by tempting Adam and Eve into knowledge, Satan's apparently evil behaviour causes 'immeasurably greater benefits for man than could conceivably have been otherwise obtained'.[17] Satan's fall becomes an act of self-sacrifice equivalent to Milton's risking heresy for the benefit of mankind. Satan cannot truly benefit by his actions, as he is barred from redemption, just as Milton cannot be benefited by his potentially heretical poetry, and yet both bring the rest of humanity closer to Grace. Both are a necessary fall.

In this introduction I have sought to define the terms of discussion for the rest of the book. The idea of the divided poet figure, at once fallen and exalted, as well as the concept of the necessary fall, are the key 'Miltonic ideas of the Fall' to which I shall refer from here on. In the discussion that follows, my arguments will rest heavily on these ideas, taking into account their impact on Romantic poets and novelists, and their own understanding of what it means to fall.

## Notes

1 Lucy Newlyn, *Paradise Lost and the Romantic Reader* (Oxford: Oxford University Press, 1993), p. 1.
2 John Milton, *Paradise Lost*, ed. by Gordon Teskey (London: Norton, 2005), 5. 20–23. All subsequent line references are from this edition, abbreviated as '*PL*', and are given in parentheses after quotations in the text.
3 William Blake, 'The Marriage of Heaven and Hell', in *William Blake: The Complete Poems*, ed. by Alicia Ostriker (New York: Penguin, 1977), 21. 23. All subsequent plate and line references are from this edition, abbreviated as '*MHH*', and are given in parentheses after quotations in the text.
4 William Poole, *Milton and the Idea of the Fall* (Cambridge: Cambridge University Press, 2005), p. 195.
5 Arthur O. Lovejoy, 'Milton and the Paradox of the Fortunate Fall', *ELH*, 4: 3 (1937), 161–79 (170).
6 David Morse, *The Age of Virtue* (Basingstoke: Palgrave, 2000), p. 280.
7 Michael Lieb, *The Dialectics of Creation: Patterns of Birth & Regeneration in Paradise Lost* (Massachusetts: University of Massachusetts Press, 1970), pp. 38–40.

8 Frank Kermode, ‘Adam Unparadised’, in *The Living Milton: Essays by Various Hands*, ed. by Frank Kermode (London: Routledge, 1960), pp. 99–120 (p. 106).
9 Peter C. Herman, *Destabilizing Milton: “Paradise Lost” and the Poetics of Incertitude* (New York: Palgrave MacMillan, 2005), p. 86.
10 John Milton, *The Readie and Easie Way* (London: 1660), VII, p. 426. ≤http://eebo.chadwyck.com/?SOURCE=pgimages.cfg&ACTION=ByID&ID=V99567≥ [accessed July 2024]
11 Catherine Bates, ‘No Sin but Irony: Kierkegaard and Milton’s Satan’, *Literature & Theology*, 1 (1997), 1–26 (5).
12 John Milton, *The Areopagitica: A Speech for the Liberty of Unlicensed Printing* (London: MacMillan, 1904), p. 1.
13 Sigmund Freud, ‘Creative Writers and Day-Dreaming’, in *Poetry in Theory: An Anthology 1900–2000*, ed. by Jon Cook (Oxford: Blackwell Publishing Ltd., 2004), pp. 41–6 (p. 42).
14 William Poole, *Milton and the Idea of the Fall* (Cambridge: Cambridge University Press, 2005), p. 178.
15 John Milton, *The Art of Logic* (London: 1673), p. 195, cited in William Poole, *Milton and the Idea of the Fall* (Cambridge: Cambridge University Press, 2005), p. 168.
16 William Poole, *Milton and the Idea of the Fall* (Cambridge: Cambridge University Press, 2005), p. 169.
17 Arthur O. Lovejoy, ‘Milton and the Paradox of the Fortunate Fall’, *ELH*, 4: 3 (1937), 161–79 (p. 163).

# Part I

# Romantic Poets' Responses to Miltonic Ideas of the Fall

In *Milton and the Revolutionary Reader* (1994), Sharron Achinstein describes Milton as 'a writer who shaped his audience not only by his principles and ideas, but by his imaginings'.[1] In the Introduction, I described how Milton employed his considerable imagination in *Paradise Lost*, creating a frame to explore the role of the poet, while using the failed revolution of Satan as a means of contending with the failure of a contemporary revolution to which he was intellectually and emotionally committed. In Part I, I will explore how these same ideas 'shape' an audience that Milton could not have been cognisant of: the Romantic poets.

In the first chapter, I will focus my attention on Blake, Coleridge, and Wordsworth, before turning to Byron and Keats in Chapter 2. In each chapter I will concentrate on one or two key works of each poet that I feel best represents that writer's use of Miltonic ideas of the Fall, while also providing some wider discussion about the specific historical contexts in which each piece was written and the bearing this has on my reading of these texts as responses to 'revolutions'. In so doing, I hope to reveal how these first- and second-generation Romantics adopted and adapted Milton's ideas of the Fall to new, though similar, ends.

## Note

1 Sharron Achinstein, *Milton and the Revolutionary Reader* (Princeton: Princeton University Press, 1994), p. 8.

DOI: 10.4324/9781003527466-2

# 1 First-Generation Romantics

## Revolutionary Responses to Miltonic Ideas of the Fall

The responses of the first-generation Romantics—specifically Wordsworth, Coleridge, and Blake—to Milton and *Paradise Lost* are curious. Their styles of poetry and prose are typically dissimilar, and their philosophies often tend to contradict one another. And yet, time and again, all of these poets are seen to draw upon Milton's work as a source of inspiration for their poetry. In my view, it is their mutual experience of political revolutions which connects these poets, and perhaps more potently, the failure of these revolutions to realise each man's hopes. John Milton was a great supporter of the Parliamentarians during the English Civil War, and of the Commonwealth and Protectorate after it. Ultimately, however, he lived to witness the reinstatement of the monarchy, and thus the failure of the republican government he had wished for. Likewise, the Romantic poets began their careers as passionate advocates of the French Revolution—and republicanism in general—but were forced to witness the political idealism of the revolution's beginnings turn into an increasingly bloody and ideologically twisted conflict.

What I will argue here is that this mutual disappointment in the failure of revolution is reflected in a common preoccupation with fallenness in the poetry of both Milton and the first-generation Romantics. In particular, I will seek to demonstrate how the first-generation Romantics express their anxiety about the political role of the poet in a post-revolutionary age through their engagement with Miltonic ideas of the Fall.

The link between the political concerns of Milton and the Romantics is one that has long been recognised by academics. Sir Herbert Grierson wrote the following in his book, *Milton & Wordsworth: Poets and Prophets* (1937):

> If we reflect on the possible experiences of a poet like Milton, Blake or Wordsworth, in passing through a revolution, a man of deep sensibilities, of active intellectual and imaginative reactions to the sensations and emotions which his temperament make so acute, and, finally, endowed with the power to express, to communicate to others, what he feels and thinks [...] One thing is certain – the high hopes, the passionate agitations which the first movement of sympathy with a great effort to renew the life of a

DOI: 10.4324/9781003527466-3

> people arouses will be followed by an acute reaction, a profound sense of disillusionment.[1]

Here, Grierson draws a direct link between poets and revolution. Indeed, he suggests an inevitability about the relationship—firstly that they will have strong feelings about revolution, and will be compelled to express those feelings, and secondly that they will ultimately be left bitterly disappointed by the outcome.

Grierson's thinking may have been influenced by his own experience. He acknowledges as much in his book, pointing to Turkey, Russia, and Spain as examples of contemporary revolutions which appeared to promise 'mutual goodwill' before turning to 'frightful consequences'.[2] And yet, it would be foolish to dismiss his argument as anachronistic or founded on personal prejudice. The essence of his argument is useful; that Milton and the first-generation Romantics react so strongly to revolution because they each see the role of the poet as being politically significant.

## William Blake: Poetry as Rebellion—Reconciling Blake and Milton

If we turn first to William Blake, we see that his poetry is heavy with both revolutionary zeal and the influence of John Milton. What I wish to demonstrate here, however, is how the nature of Blake's revolutionary spirit changes over time and how this manifests itself in his poetry through his engagement with Miltonic ideas of the Fall. In order to do this, I shall compare Blake's *The Marriage of Heaven and Hell* (1790) and *Milton* (1804), arguing that one can perceive a marked process of moderation between the two poems, as Blake moves from a position which appears to endorse violent rebellion towards a more nuanced, intellectual position, which I shall elucidate as the discussion develops.

*The Marriage of Heaven and Hell* was composed in the optimistic first few years of the French Revolution, only a year after the fall of the Bastille. Richard Cronin suggests that the poem 'decisively signals Blake's progression [...] to "political radicalism"'.[3] It is certainly true that the poem reflects Blake's initial enthusiasm for revolution. This can most clearly be seen in 'A Song of Liberty', the final section of *The Marriage*. In this short piece of highly bombastic rhetoric, Blake urges France to 'rend down thy dungeon' and Spain to 'burst the barriers of Old Rome' (*MHH*, 25. 6–8). Indeed, the poem as a whole is very much concerned with the destruction of old frameworks, both physical and mental.

In particular, the poem engages with Emmanuel Swedenborg's *Heaven and Hell* (1758), in which Swedenborg proposes an innate conflict between the binaries of man's 'hereditary Evil' and the goodness of God.[4] Swedenborg posits that humanity must allow God to act through it, and essentially to resist its own nature to achieve 'goodness'. Blake disrupts this philosophy entirely, arguing that Swedenborg's assertions are based on a fundamental misunderstanding of morality, writing that:

> Without Contraries is no progression. Attraction and
> Repulsion, Reason and Energy, Love and Hate, are
> necessary to Human existence.
>
> (*MHH*, 3. 7–9)

It seems apparent, then, that at this stage in his career, before the 'first movement of sympathy' with the French Revolution has dissipated, Blake is not especially concerned with any Miltonic idea of fallenness. As Jean H. Hagstrum puts it, Blake at this stage of his career conceives only that 'revolution means action, and action envisages violence', rendering the biblical Fall a nonsense.[5] If it is better to 'murder an infant in the cradle than nurse unacted desires' (*MHH*, 10. 7), then the impulse to eat a piece of fruit cannot be a meaningful expression of sin.

When Blake writes, then, that Milton was of the 'Devil's party/ Without knowing it' (*MHH*, 5. 23), we can read this as simply being part of Blake's wider intention of discrediting old modes of thought or understanding. Blake does not read *Paradise Lost* as being deliberately engaged in a subversive examination of the awkward relationship between good and evil, but as a work that merely falls into these ideas by accident while delivering an otherwise orthodox sermon.

What makes this such a potent criticism is Blake's view of the poet as an 'artist-prophet', with an active role in responding to 'social and political evil'.[6] In one of his 'Memorable Fancies', Blake depicts a conversation between himself and the prophet Isaiah:

> I asked: does a firm perswasion that a thing is so, make it so?
> He replied. All poets believe that it does, & in ages of imagination this firm perswasion removed mountains; but many are not capable of a firm perswasion of anything.
>
> (*MHH*, 12. 10–16)

Milton, in Blake's eyes, does not meet Isaiah's criteria for the poet/artist-prophet. If he is on one hand justifying the ways of 'God to Men', and on the other a member of the 'Devil's party', then he cannot be of a 'firm perswasion'. For Blake, *Paradise Lost* cannot succeed in its stated aim of justifying or explaining God to its readers because, to Blake, Milton's orthodox message is betrayed by his unconsciously subversive spirit.

It is not until later that we see Blake seriously reassess his understanding of Milton and *Paradise Lost*. Ian Balfour rightly observes that 'No other Romantic poet confronts Milton so directly' as when Blake writes *Milton*.[7] The poem is, like *The Marriage of Heaven and Hell*, a response to *Paradise Lost*. And yet the nature of the response is different, although both texts appear to share a revolutionary theme. In the preface to *Milton* we find Blake very much invested in a rabble-rousing form of rhetoric:

> Rouze up O Young Men of the New Age!
> set your foreheads against the ignorant Hirelings! For we have
> Hirelings in the Camp, the Court & the University:
> who would if they could, forever depress the Mental and
> prolong Corporeal War.[8]

And yet, even this apparent commonality with *The Marriage* belies a subtle point of difference. Whereas in *The Marriage* Blake is urging the French to cast down their dungeon in what seems a very physical sense, here we see a deliberate appeal to shift the focus from the 'Corporeal' to the 'Mental', suggesting he has at least partially 'embraced Milton's course' in *Paradise Lost* and rendered the conflict 'solely a "mental fight"'.[9] In *The Marriage*, Blake is swift to mock those who see a binary division between 'Reason' and 'Energy', the 'passive' and the 'active' (*MHH,* 3. 11–12), and so this acknowledgement of the separation of mind and body appears a significant move towards a more moderate, considered stance.

It is notable that in this condemnation of violence the French Revolution is never addressed in direct terms. Rather than attack those anonymous, warmongering 'Hirelings', Blake chooses instead to vent his fury upon the 'silly Greek and Latin slaves of the sword' (*M*, 1. 10). One could suggest that this is simply Blake's way of avoiding talking about politics in direct terms—perhaps being wary of charges of sedition. Ian Balfour, however, sees the reference to Greek and Latin as a direct reflection of Blake's dislike of the epic, specifically 'the war epic of Homer and his imitators'.[10] Balfour cites an appendix to *The Prophetic Books*, entitled 'On Virgil', in support of this claim. In it, Blake quotes a line from the *Aeneid*: 'Let others study Art: Rome has somewhat better to do, namely War and Dominion'. Blake goes on to criticise Virgil, Homer, and Ovid directly, suggesting that their work is undermined by the militancy of its cultural origin: 'Rome and Greece swept Art into their maw and destroyed it; a warlike State never can produce Art'.[11]

In his poetry, Blake thrives on ideas of conflict and collision, but he sees war as the antithesis of art. Herbert Tucker suggests that Blake, particularly in *Milton*, deliberately seeks to subvert the classical tradition of the epic as a celebration of violence by investing the 'virtues of strife', such as heroism and bravery, 'in arts and peace'.[12] In writing *Milton* as an epic, but without the warlike themes of Homer, Blake is simultaneously seeking to redeem that form of poetry along with the higher ideals of the French Revolution, both of which he deems to have been marred by war.

That, of course, is why *Paradise Lost* and John Milton are both the model and the subject of Blake's poem. *Paradise Lost* is an epic unlike most others in that it is very much about 'Mental'—as opposed to 'Corporeal'—conflict. Indeed, the only violence has already taken place, described by the Angel Raphael in Book Five as the 'invisible exploits/ Of warring Spirits' (*PL*, 5. 565–566). As for choosing Milton as the hero, Balfour speculates that 'Blake felt compelled to summon back Milton' because he was 'a poet for whom prophecy and poetry were virtually identical'.[13] This, too, seems to represent a change from the Blake who wrote *The Marriage*—since in that poem there are very few voices that are clearly attributed to specific speakers. Even in the section entitled 'The Voice of the Devil', it is not made explicit whether what follows is meant to be literally read as the voice of Satan. In *Milton*, however, there are three dominant, well-defined voices: the epic narrator, the Bard, and Milton.

J. Bronowski wisely makes the point that attempting to attribute any particular line in Blake's poetry to a particular source or voice is rarely as straightforward as it might appear. In making this point, he directs us to the sheer diversity of influences present in Blake:

> the more symbols we find Blake to have picked up, and the more random their sources, the plainer it becomes that he took them less by choice than by habit. All these symbols were alike to Blake, because all were to him shadows of the same mystery.[14]

However, in a sense this is what makes *Milton* so interesting. Although it contains all of the seeming 'randomness' that Bronowski identifies, it is relatively singular among Blake's works in its adherence to form, specifically the epic form. This is significant, as the epic has at its core a well-defined set of voices and characters—the epic narrator and the hero being the most fundamental.

Earlier, I suggested that in *Paradise Lost* Milton used this clear division of voices to illustrate the two conflicting aspects of the poet: the prophetic, divine side and the fallen side. I believe that Blake does something very similar, but for a different purpose. Not only is Blake's sense of fallenness more explicitly bound up in a sense of political defeat, but it is also more morally complex. Milton wishes to justify the ways of God to men, and to find a way to explain how the sins of mankind might be part of wider context leading to a greater good. Blake's intentions are less easily defined and rationalised. Not only does he see his role as less reflective and more active—a 'shaper of myth', as Northrop Frye would have it, who 'holds in his hands the thunderbolts that destroy one society and create another'—he also does not see any useful distinction between the 'contraries' of good and evil.[15] In this sense, *Milton's* purpose is antithetical to *Paradise Lost*. Whereas the latter seeks to express morality in binary terms, the former looks to collapse these binaries and create something new. *Milton*, in this sense, is a journey that sees the two 'contraries' of William Blake and John Milton, the radical and the Puritan, transform and unify.

At the beginning of the poem, we find 'Milton' dissatisfied but uncomplaining: 'Unhappy tho in heav'n, he obey'd, he murmur'd not' (*M*, 2. 18). For Blake, this is sinfulness incarnate, the nursing of 'unacted desires'. In contrast we have the 'loud voic'd Bard' (*M*, 14. 9), an extension of the epic narrator, who sings without caution. The Bard is certain of his own authority as one privy to the 'inspiration of Poetic Genius' (*M*, 14. 1). This is something of an inversion of *Paradise Lost*, where the narrator has a reserved voice, interjecting at points to bemoan Satan's lack of humility. In *Milton*, the narrator unashamedly boasts of his own power: 'I am Inspired! I know it is Truth! for I Sing' (*M*, 13. 51).

Ultimately, the Bard moves 'Milton' to fall from heaven to purge his own orthodoxy. Mirroring Blake's lines in *The Marriage*, 'Milton' declares: 'I am in my Selfhood that Satan: I am that Evil One!' (*M*, 14. 30). As the epic continues, 'Milton' joins and interacts with different people and objects, including Blake's foot and his own 'hermaphroditic' shadow (*M*, 140. 37). Any trace of the restrictive, 'sensible' voice of *Paradise Lost*'s narrator is gone.

My argument, then, that *Milton* represents a shift towards moderation, requires further justification. Blake may begin with an orthodox epic framework and an orthodox hero, but he swiftly undermines them and leads us back into his familiar state of imaginative anarchy. However, although the images and symbols Blake draws upon are strange and incompatible, they are not mindless. As Bronowski suggests, they serve a direct purpose:

> Blake himself knew that, at the bottom, his symbolism is held together only by his energy and his imaginative insight. For Blake was not trying to puzzle out a secret or a system. He was trying to make men give up systems, rationalist and religious alike.[16]

What Bronowski identifies here is, in a sense, Blake's political manifesto—the undermining of restrictive systems of government and belief. And yet, what I find to be so significant about *Milton* is not that it undermines these systems, but that it undermines them through poetry. Milton is not violently coerced by the Bard, but rather persuaded through song. 'Milton' doesn't return to the Earth as a warlike scourge, but instead as one reproving the nations of Earth for their 'warlike Selfhood' (*M*, 14. 16).

Although Blake is disillusioned by the outcome of the French Revolution, his principles are not altered or diminished as a result, but rather strengthened.

As Balfour reminds us, Blake always professed an 'abhorrence of war', but in *The Marriage of Heaven and Hell* it seemed he was prepared to sacrifice this principle.[17] In *Milton*, none of the goals have changed—the orthodox establishment is still clearly defined as the enemy—but the methods Blake is prepared to employ to combat it have been refined. In *Paradise Lost* he finds his model, a 'poem that broke with tradition as much as it followed it' and delivered its message without recourse to war.[18] *Milton* is Blake's homage to this concept, and his blueprint for all future revolutions. As Hagstrum warns us, it 'would be a profound mistake' to read Blake's transition to a mode of 'mental fight' as a move to 'quietistic piety'.[19] Instead, by providing an artistic, poetic alternative to the physical conflict of revolution, Blake creates a political role for the poet which abstracts itself from the baseness of partisanship and violence while retaining every ounce of his 'prophetic anger'.[20]

## Coleridge: Retrospective Conservatism and the Intervening Voice

Like Blake, Samuel Taylor Coleridge was undoubtedly moved by the French Revolution to the 'high hopes' and 'passionate agitations' that Grierson writes about, and equally hurt by the inevitable sense of disillusionment that followed. However, Coleridge's reaction to this disillusionment differs significantly from Blake's. Whereas Blake remains ideologically consistent in his politics, the 'ultimate failure of the French Revolution' leads to a 'collapse of [Coleridge's] hopes for the improvement of mankind by political action'.[21] In his influential essay, 'Coleridge, the French Revolution, and "The Ancient Mariner": Collective Guilt and Individual Salvation' (1989), Kitson posits that this disillusionment manifests itself in a retreat into nature—an eschewing of direct political engagement in favour of a somewhat nebulous faith in 'the agency of natural forces'.[22]

I would like to go further than Kitson and suggest that the older Coleridge not only discards his youthful radicalism, but that he actively pursues a distinct form of political and poetic conservatism. Furthermore, I will argue that Coleridge can be seen to impose his later, increasingly conservative values onto the poetry of his more radical past, using *Paradise Lost* and Miltonic ideas of the Fall as his model for doing so. This captures a fundamental change in Coleridge's view of the political role of the poet—moving from a position which holds poetry to be a vehicle for change to one that is increasingly concerned with supporting the status quo.

In 'France, An Ode' (1798) Coleridge describes what seems to be the primary catalyst for this change. In the poem, he writes of his initial jubilation when France 'Stampt'd her strong foot and said, she would be free', but swiftly points to the invasion of Switzerland by France as the moment he loses all faith in the revolution[23]:

> Forgive me, Freedom! O forgive these dreams!
> I hear thy voice, I hear thy loud lament,
> From bleak Helvetica's icy caverns sent –
> [...] forgive me, that I cherish'd
> One thought, that ever bless'd your cruel foes
>
> ('France', ll. 64–71)

Although Coleridge seeks to reaffirm his love of freedom and liberty, 'With what deep worship I have still ador'd/ The spirit of divinest liberty' ('France', ll. 20–21), it is difficult not to read a weakening of his convictions in the poem. When he writes 'O Liberty! With profitless endeavour/ Have I pursued thee many a weary hour' ('France', ll. 89–91), one is left with the deep sense that Coleridge has begun a serious re-evaluation of his principles and beliefs. A process of re-evaluation which I believe encompasses not only his politics, but also his religious and poetic ideologies, and which has a profound impact on his ideas about the role of the poet.

In this regard, the connection between Coleridge's beliefs to Milton and *Paradise* is profound, and perhaps most strongly expressed in *The Rime of the Ancient Mariner*. Returning to Kitson, he observes that:

> Coleridge had Milton's career very much in mind when writing 'The Ancient Mariner'. Like himself, the poet of *Paradise Lost* had witnessed the complete wreck of his own hopes for a regenerated nation.[24]

If we take *The Rime of the Ancyent Marinere* (1798), and its subsequent reworking, *The Rime of the Ancient Mariner* (1817), as our primary examples, it is possible to trace Coleridge's transition towards religious and poetic orthodoxy in his poetry, and how he adopts the frameworks of Milton's poem in order to express it.

When we compare the Argument of the 1798 version with the epigraph that replaces it in the latter, we see the first example of this change in Coleridge's attitudes. In the Argument of 1798 Coleridge merely describes, in simple terms, the nature of the poem—that it concerns a mariner and 'the strange things that befell' him.[25] The epigraph of 1817 is in stark contrast to this simplicity. Taken from Thomas Burnet's *Archaelogiae Philisophicae* (1692), the short quotation, written in Latin, speculates on the existence of 'invisible [...] beings' and their distinguishing 'features and functions'. The extract ends with a caution that 'we must be watchful for the truth and keep a sense of proportion'.[26] The choice of Latin is significant, as it is the traditional language of the church. One could argue that this is simply an attempt to evoke the same pre-Reformation world that we see in *Christabel* (1816): an indication that the Mariner's wisdom stems from a philosophy that in some way precludes the infighting of an increasingly diverse Christian landscape.

However, I would suggest that the purpose of the Latin epigraph is more specific than this. Marilyn Butler notes that the failure of the radical ideals of the French Revolution caused Coleridge to become increasingly conservative not only politically, but also in his religious affiliation. She points to his book, *On the Constitution of Church and State* (1830), describing it as an 'idealized, half-nostalgic portrait of how a paternalistic old system worked'—referring to the idea of both the church and the state as 'father figures'.[27] The Latin of the epigraph recalls this system, whereby a Latin-speaking priest was necessarily required as a guide and interpreter: a father figure. This, coupled with the paternal caution to 'be watchful for the truth and keep a sense of proportion', suggests Coleridge's increased appetite for authority, structure, and caution, both in society and religious belief.

In contrast to this, the young Coleridge was far more adventurous in his religious beliefs. In 'The Eolian Harp' (1795) he espouses a pantheist philosophy, roughly defined as the belief that 'God is everything and everything is God'.[28] In the poem, he speculates that all things may be animated by 'one intellectual Breeze,/ At once the soul of each, and God of all'. He does go on, however, to register some guilt over this 'unregenerate' speculation, having received from his wife's 'serious eye a mild reproof'.[29] By the time he composes the 1817 version of *The Ancient Mariner*, it is as though Coleridge has internalised his wife's disapproval and turned it on his own work. The addition of the marginal gloss to the text, as well as the modernising of some of the archaic language, such as 'Ancyent Marinere' to 'Ancient Mariner', seems to express an anxiety about a spirit of unconventionality that the author no longer fully subscribes to. Coleridge appears to have reconceptualised his role as a poet from one that is prepared to be speculative and experimental to one that is increasingly restrictive and conformist.

Given this change in attitude, it is striking that Coleridge consistently sought to define *The Ancient Mariner* in all its versions as a purely imaginative poem. He is famously quoted as having defended his poem against the accusation that it had no moral by saying:

> The only, or chief fault, if I might say so, was the obtrusion of the moral sentiment so openly on the reader as a principle or cause of action in a work of such pure imagination.[30]

In this sense, *The Ancient Mariner*, particularly in the 1817 version, shares the tension between morality and imagination that we find in *Paradise Lost*. In the original 1798 poem, Coleridge does indeed seem at pains to exercise the freedom of the imagination, leaving ambiguities open to speculation. In the latter, however, the voice of the marginal gloss does not even allow the geography to pass unremarked: 'the ship encounters the Pacific Ocean, and sails northward even till it reaches the Line' (*AM17*, p. 67). The function of this intervening voice can be seen as a reflection of the epic narrator's role in *Paradise Lost*, a curb on the 'unregenerate', or fallen, aspect of the poet figure. Conversely, the Mariner stands as a parallel to Milton's Satan. Both fit the mould of prophet—the Mariner's 'strange power of speech' (*AM98*, l. 620) and compulsion to tell his tale are a testament to this fact—and they both follow the Miltonic pattern of the necessary fall. In Satan's case he falls, and causes Adam and Eve to fall, in order that mankind can later achieve Grace. The Mariner's fall occasions a less universal redemption, that of the wedding guest, who ends the tale a 'sadder and a wiser man' (*AM98*, l. 657) for having heard the Mariner's tale. Though as James Boulger suggests in his essay, 'Christian Skepticism in the Ancient Mariner' (1965), it seems doubtless that Coleridge wants his readers to 'play the part of the wedding guest [...] and finally to share his epistemological and [...] religious anxieties'.[31]

What makes Coleridge's Miltonic self-regulation even more interesting is the political context in which he was writing. In 1817, the year in which the revised version of the *Ancient Mariner* was published in *Sibylline Leaves*, both the Treason Act and the Seditious Meetings Prevention Bill were passed. These, along with four other pieces of legislation, later known as the 'gag acts', were specifically designed to limit the freedom of political expression.[32] In this context, Coleridge's desire to retrospectively impose a conservative voice onto his poetry may be interpreted in several different ways. One could simply read his actions as a means of appeasing a repressive regime, distancing himself from his radical associations as an act of self-defence against accusations of sedition. And yet, the *Ancient Mariner* is not an explicitly political poem. Indeed, E. M. W Tillyard goes so far as to say the poem has 'a total lack of politics', which on a purely surface level one would be hard pressed to disagree with.[33] It is clear, therefore, that if Coleridge had wished only to dispel the notion of himself as a seditious poet there are more overtly controversial works which would have served this purpose better.

In my view, the reason that Coleridge uses *The Ancient Mariner* is because it allows him to confront the issue of guilt. If the transformation of his role as poet—moving from radical free-thinker to defender of the establishment—is to be credible, it is essential that Coleridge is able express his sincere regret for his former beliefs. Butler suggests that the significance of guilt in the *Ancient Mariner* lies in the parallel between Coleridge and the Mariner himself. She observes that the '*Ancient Mariner* depicts a man in whom moral isolation is inseparable from a sense of guilt'.[34] For her, Coleridge viewed his 'isolated' past as a radical in the same way as the Mariner considers his slaying of the albatross, as a mark of deeply personal shame.

However, *The Ancient Mariner* is about more than the mere expression of regret. The narrative of the poem is a parable of how sin can lead to a moral outcome for the sinner. In the case of the Mariner, his slaying of the albatross, and his subsequent guilt, leads him to understand the moral worth of 'All things both great and small' (*AM17*, l. 615). For Coleridge, his guilt over supporting the French Revolution is what leads him to become the stalwart defender of political stability we see in *On the Constitution of Church and State*. Coleridge's 'retelling' of the poem, with its clear moral message, mirrors the actions of the Mariner himself, who repeats his own story in order to atone for his past. As Kitson rightly states in the conclusion to his own essay, 'Without the experience of the Revolution, "The Ancient Mariner" would not be the poem it is'.[35] In effect, the message of the poem reflects that of *Paradise Lost*: that sometimes a fall is necessary to occasion a greater moral outcome.

*The Ancient Mariner*, then, is a poem thoroughly rooted in *Paradise Lost* and Miltonic ideas of the Fall. The 1817 version has a division of voices comparable to Satan and the epic narrator, and both versions address the idea of the necessary fall. Both *Paradise Lost* and *The Ancient Mariner* confront the issue of the role of the poet, but in significantly different ways. *Paradise Lost* addresses the evangelical function of poetry, and whether the poet is an appropriate agent for religious philosophy, whereas *The Ancient Mariner* engages with the topic on a level which is more personal to its author. The redemption of the Mariner, along with his ongoing suffering, bears a direct comparison with Coleridge's own experiences. In this sense, *The Ancient Mariner*, and the changes which he makes to it, are more about Coleridge's individual relationship with poetry, as opposed to the more general engagement with the role of the poet we see in *Paradise Lost*.

At this point, it is worth reflecting on another poet who had a great influence on Coleridge—William Wordsworth—whose work provides us with a deeper understanding of the first-generation Romantics' shared preoccupation with Milton.

## Wordsworth: 'Two Consciousnesses' and the Consummation of the Poet's Mind

Like Coleridge, William Wordsworth was deeply affected by the French Revolution. However, unlike Coleridge, Wordsworth actually lived in France in the early 1790s. Nicholas Roe notes how the first-hand nature of Wordsworth's contact with the French Revolution had a profound impact on his political sensibilities, suggesting that his 'political radicalism was bound up with his personal experience of revolution and responsive to its changing course'.[36] In this part of the chapter I will focus on Wordsworth's autobiographical epic poem, *The Prelude* (1805), arguing that its narrative about the growth and 'consummation of the Poet's mind' is directly linked to Wordsworth's experience of the revolution, and to his evolving political ideologies.[37] I will suggest that he draws directly upon *Paradise Lost*, and the Miltonic idea of the split poetic identity, to make an explicit distinction between his pre- and post-revolutionary selves, not only in terms of his changed political allegiances, but also his changed views on his role as a poet.

Very early on in *The Prelude,* Wordsworth introduces the idea of a strong division between his past and present selves. Indeed, he recalls his time as a schoolboy as if literally reflecting upon the life of a different person:

> [...] so wide appears
> The vacancy between me and those days
> Which yet have such self-presence in my mind
> That, sometimes, when I think of it, I
> Seem two consciousnesses, conscious of myself
> And of some other Being
>
> (*TP*, II. 28–33)

It is, in my view, the French Revolution which separates these two consciousnesses, with the failure of the revolution representing a kind of fall for Wordsworth—a loss of innocence which fundamentally alters his political and poetic outlook. In the words of a contemporary review of the poem, the revolution and its aftermath delivers 'an electric shock to his whole spiritual being' which moved him to 'mediate deeply on the [...] powers and duties of the poet; [and] upon the relations of society and nature'.[38] This shock draws him away from a position of radical idealism towards a more anxious conservatism, the form of which echoes that of Coleridge as described earlier. For me, it is this political transition which is the key distinction between the two 'consciousnesses' which Wordsworth describes.

It may seem strange to suggest that Wordsworth frames his childhood self in a political context—when he talks about the 'Sly subterfuge' (*TP*, II. 106) of his childish escapades it is generally in reference to the breaking of petty rules rather than the overthrow of governments. However, I would make the case that the mischievous schoolboy and the political radical are merely different stages upon the same trajectory, and that Wordsworth is deliberately framing this political radicalism as emerging from a childish sensibility. Indeed, in Book IX of *The Prelude* Wordsworth makes an explicit connection between his childhood, and indeed his childhood reading of poetry, with his pre-revolutionary politics:

> Though untaught by thinking or by books [...]
> Tales of Poets, [...] made my heart
> Beat high and fill'd my fancy with fair forms,
> Old heroes and their sufferings and their deeds;
> Yet in the regal Sceptre, and the pomp
> Of Orders and Degrees, I nothing found
> Then, or had ever, even in crudest youth,
> That dazzled me; but rather what my soul
> Mourn'd for, or loath'd, beholding that the best
> Rul'd not, and feeling that they ought to rule.
>
> (*TP*, IX. 209–215)

He goes on to write that, as a child, he was predisposed to 'the government of equal rights', and that he was already a 'Republican' before he ever went to France (*TP*, IX. 230–248). Wordsworth seems to be suggesting, then, that his radical, republican ideology began in his 'crudest youth', and that poetry was a significant factor in its development. As a young man, he appears to have seen poetry as serving a heroic function. Indeed, he seems to dismiss the idea of monarchy purely on the basis that regal 'pomp' does not capture his imagination in the way that the grand poetic narratives of 'deeds' and 'sufferings' are able to.

While Wordsworth does not explicitly dismiss these pre-revolutionary attitudes as foolish, his association of them with childhood is in some regards a direct critique. Wordsworth is generally regarded as fostering an 'idealizing, nostalgic', typically Romantic view of childhood that imbues children themselves with an apparently 'ideology-proof, organic sensibility' rooted in nature. Although this carries a host of more positive connotations, it also bears with it a suggestion of political innocence rising to the level of naivety.[39]

We see this expressed more clearly in Wordsworth's 'Essay Supplementary to Preface' (1815). Here, Wordsworth gives an account of poetry and the reading public throughout history, touching specifically on the inherent dangers of a youthful perspective. The tone of the piece is fiercely didactic—David Duff describes it at as an effort 'to tell us how to read, and how *not* to read', with particular emphasis on the latter.[40] Wordsworth is particularly keen to warn his younger readers, 'who in nothing can escape illusion', about the dangerous passions that poetry can arouse:

> what temptations to go astray are here held forth for them whose thoughts have been little disciplined by the understanding, and whose feelings revolt from the sway of reason![41]

This reference to minds 'little disciplined by the understanding' is reminiscent of Wordsworth's description of his younger self, 'untaught by thinking or by books'. It seems that in the post-revolutionary period Wordsworth is far more wary of the seductively grand narratives of poetry. In addition, his position on the role of the poet has changed. As a youth he appears to have been inspired by poets to emulate the 'deeds' of 'Old heroes', and to indulge his flights of fancy. In 1815—in the wake of the French Revolution and the Napoleonic Wars—he is using his own position as a poet to discourage exactly that kind of behaviour.

As I have been suggesting, the cause of this profound alteration was Wordsworth's reaction to the failure of the French Revolution, particularly the increasingly savage violence of the Terror. When Wordsworth describes this period in *The Prelude,* it is in stark, almost apocalyptic terms:

> The goaded land waxed mad; the crimes of a few
> Spread into madness of the many; blasts
> From hell came sanctified like airs from heaven.

> The sternness of the Just, the faith of those
> Who doubted not that Providence had times
> Of anger and of vengeance, theirs who throned
> The human understanding paramount
> And made of that their god, the hopes of those
> Who were content to barter short-lived pangs
> For a paradise of angels, the blind-rage
> Of insolent tempters.
>
> (*TP*, X. 312–326)

Later on in *The Prelude*, Wordsworth acknowledges that, in the aftermath of all this bloodshed, a 'shock had then been given/ To old opinions', and that his mind was 'let loose' from his former beliefs (*TP*, X. 860–863), bespeaking a 'unique [and personal] experience and its psychological aftermath, rather than a distant empathy' predicated on an abstract sympathy with the afflicted.[42] It is in this period of shock that the 'two consciousnesses' of Wordsworth are formed. The naive, pre-revolutionary version of himself that had absolute faith in the 'mighty scheme of truth' that only poets and prophets are 'enabled to perceive', is replaced by a more conservative, post-revolutionary self who has witnessed first-hand the dangers of his former political grandiosity and self-mythologising (*TP*, XII, 302–304).

In this sense, the relationship between Wordsworth's 'two consciousness' in *The Prelude* is comparable to the Satan/epic narrator relationship in *Paradise Lost.* In both instances there are two competing voices, one compelled by passion and instinct, the other by sober consideration, with the latter acting as a curb on the former. Other critics have also commented on this Miltonic dynamic. Willard Spiegelman makes a direct comparison between the pre-revolutionary Wordsworth and Satan, suggesting that the description of his character 'is riddled with suggestions of malice [...] with muted echoes of satanic fall and vengeance'.[43] There is a good example of this in Book I, where Wordsworth describes his childhood self as a 'fell destroyer', capable of being led astray by passions that 'O'erpowere'd [...] better reason' (*TP*, I. 318–326). In contrast to this, at the end of *The Prelude* Wordsworth imagines his and Coleridge's future roles as poets in almost priestly terms:

> Prophets of Nature, we to them will speak
> A lasting inspiration, sanctified
> By reason and by truth; what we have loved
> Others will love; and we may teach them how;
> Instruct them how the mind of man becomes
> A thousand times more beautiful than the earth
> On which he dwells, above this Frame of things
> (Which mid all revolutions in the hopes
> And fears of men, doth still remain unchanged).
>
> (*TP*, XIII. 435–443)

In this passage, Wordsworth is no longer a destroyer, but a pedagogue. By highlighting the sanctity of reason—the quality which he struggled to master as a child—he emphasises the flaw in his younger self's character which led him into political radicalism. As Roe puts it, Wordsworth becomes both his 'own Satan as he is his own redeemer', rendering *The Prelude* doubly Miltonic.[44] Not only does this division embody the split poet figure we find in *Paradise Lost*, but it also illustrates how the failure of the French Revolution was a necessary fall in the growth and 'consummation' of Wordsworth's true 'Poet's mind' (*TP*, XIII. 264). Without the violent shock of the Terror, Wordsworth would not have reassessed his political and poetical ideologies, or as he refers to them: 'the errors into which I was betray'd' (*TP*, X. 881–886). Without this fall he would have remained the same man who wrote, in a letter to the Bishop of Llandaff, that in order for Liberty to 'reign in peace [she] must establish herself in violence'.[45] He would, in effect, have remained a poet ruled by childish passion and instinct, rather than by understanding and reason, and could not, therefore, be a fit guide to the next generation.

Indeed, this desire to pass on poetic wisdom seems to be central to Wordsworth's re-conceptualisation of his role as a poet. I have already pointed to the heavily didactic 'Essay Supplementary to the Preface' as an example of Wordsworth in his role as a poet/teacher. Duff suggests that adopting this pedagogic guise is a deliberate strategy on the part of Wordsworth to insinuate himself into the political and literary establishment. His keenness to instruct the public on the proper way to read poetry in the 'Essay' is a 'defensive as well as assertive' gesture; insulating him from the potential 'misreading' of his early poetry, written under 'very different historical circumstances and with different ideological motives'.[46] In this regard, *The Prelude* itself serves a similar function, in that it prevents a 'misreading' of Wordsworth himself. He makes the Miltonic division between his two 'consciousnesses' as stark as possible, so that his readers will not judge the Wordsworth of the post-revolutionary period by the words and actions of the pre-revolutionary Wordsworth.

The purpose of *The Prelude*, then, is to describe Wordsworth's transition from a youth—inspired by the heroic glamour of poetry into supporting an uprising he was ill equipped to understand—to a mature poet who is chastened by his experiences but wiser as a result. In framing his narrative in this way, Wordsworth seeks to justify himself as a valid political voice to those who are wary of his former radicalism. In this, his actions resemble Coleridge's attempts to impose his new conservative voice onto his old poetry. Both poets seek to prove that their disavowal of the French Revolution is more than a hypocritical act of convenience, but a real and significant change in their political and poetical philosophies. The Miltonic ideas of the split poet figure, and of the necessary fall, provide them with a compelling framework in which to make this argument—an explicit source which all of the poets discussed here are united in drawing upon.

I began this chapter by asserting that each of the first-generation Romantics shared a political sensibility with Milton; a sensibility that expressed itself in an anxious preoccupation with fallenness. What I have tried to do subsequently is demonstrate how, for each of these poets, the French Revolution was ineluctably tied to this anxiety. The failure of this political uprising to match their expectations forced a change in all of them, both political and poetical. In the case of William Blake this change was subtle but significant, not altering his political and ideological aspirations, but transforming his sense of how these aims ought to be achieved. For Coleridge and Wordsworth, it was fundamental. Indeed, the alteration it elicited in these latter two was so powerful that it had profound implications for the generation of poets that followed them.

## Notes

1 Herbert Grierson, *Milton & Wordsworth: Poets and Prophets* (London: Cambridge University Press, 1937), p. 147.
2 Herbert Grierson, *Milton & Wordsworth: Poets and Prophets* (London: Cambridge University Press, 1937), p. 147.
3 Richard Cronin, *The Politics of Romantic Poetry. In Search of the Pure Commonwealth* (Basingstoke: Palgrave MacMillan, 2000), p. 50.
4 Andrew M. Stauffer, Marilyn Butler, and James Chandler, *Anger, Revolution, and Romanticism* (Cambridge: Cambridge University Press, 2005), p. 81.
5 Jean H. Hagstrum, '"The Wrath of the Lamb": A Study of William Blake's Conversations', in *From Sensibility to Romanticism: Essays Presented to Frederick A. Pottle*, ed. by Frederick W. Hilles and Harold Bloom (Oxford: Oxford University Press, 1965), pp. 311–330 (p. 321).
6 Jean H. Hagstrum, '"The Wrath of the Lamb": A Study of William Blake's Conversations', in *From Sensibility to Romanticism: Essays Presented to Frederick A. Pottle*, ed. by Frederick W. Hilles and Harold Bloom (Oxford: Oxford University Press, 1965), pp. 311–30 (p. 316).
7 Ian Balfour, *The Rhetoric of Romantic Prophecy* (Stanford: Stanford University Press, 2002), p. 156.
8 William Blake, 'Milton', in *William Blake: the Complete Poems,* ed. by Alicia Ostriker (New York: Penguin, 1977), 1. 11–15. All subsequent plate and line references are from this addition, abbreviated as '*M*', and are given in parentheses after quotations in the text.
9 Jean H. Hagstrum, '"The Wrath of the Lamb": A Study of William Blake's Conversations', in *From Sensibility to Romanticism: Essays Presented to Frederick A. Pottle*, ed. by Frederick W. Hilles and Harold Bloom (Oxford: Oxford University Press, 1965), pp. 311–30 (p. 324).
10 Ian Balfour, *The Rhetoric of Romantic Prophecy* (Stanford: Stanford University Press, 2002), p. 146.
11 William Blake, 'On Virgil', Appendix to *The Prophetic Books*, ll. 5–8. http://www.bartleby.com/235/343.html [accessed July 2024]
12 Herbert Tucker, *Epic: Britain's Heroic Muse 1790–1910* (Oxford: Oxford University Press, 2008), p. 105.
13 Ian Balfour, *The Rhetoric of Romantic Prophecy* (Stanford: Stanford University Press, 2002), p. 154.
14 J. Bronowski, *William Blake and the Age of Revolution* (London: Routledge, 1972), p. 32.
15 Northrop Frye, 'Blake After Two Centuries', in *English Romantic Poets: Modern Essays in Criticism*, ed. by M. H. Abrams (Oxford: Oxford University Press, 1966), pp. 55–67 (p. 64).

16 J. Bronowski, *William Blake and the Age of Revolution* (London: Routledge, 1972), p. 31.
17 Ian Balfour, *The Rhetoric of Romantic Prophecy* (Stanford: Stanford University Press, 2002), p. 141.
18 Ian Balfour, *The Rhetoric of Romantic Prophecy* (Stanford: Stanford University Press, 2002), p. 147.
19 Jean H. Hagstrum, '"The Wrath of the Lamb": A Study of William Blake's Conversations', in *From Sensibility to Romanticism: Essays Presented to Frederick A. Pottle*, ed. by Frederick W. Hilles and Harold Bloom (Oxford: Oxford University Press, 1965), pp. 311–30 (p. 326).
20 Jean H. Hagstrum, '"The Wrath of the Lamb": A Study of William Blake's Conversations', in *From Sensibility to Romanticism: Essays Presented to Frederick A. Pottle*, ed. by Frederick W. Hilles and Harold Bloom (Oxford: Oxford University Press, 1965), pp. 311–30 (p. 326).
21 Peter Kitson, 'Coleridge, the French Revolution, and "The Ancient Mariner": Collective Guilt and Individual Salvation', *The Yearbook of English Studies*, 19 (1989), 197–207 (197).
22 Peter Kitson, 'Coleridge, the French Revolution, and "The Ancient Mariner": Collective Guilt and Individual Salvation', *The Yearbook of English Studies*, 19 (1989), 197–207 (206).
23 Samuel Taylor Coleridge, 'France, an Ode', in *Coleridge's Poetry and Prose*, ed. by Nicholas Halmi, Paul Magnuson and Raimonda Modiano (London: Norton, 2004), l. 4. All subsequent line references are from this edition, abbreviated as 'France', and are given in parentheses after quotations in the text.
24 Peter Kitson, 'Coleridge, the French Revolution, and "The Ancient Mariner": Collective Guilt and Individual Salvation', *The Yearbook of English Studies*, 19 (1989), 197–207 (197).
25 Samuel Taylor Coleridge, 'The Rime of the Ancyent Marinere', in *Coleridge's Poetry and Prose*, ed. by Nicholas Halmi, Paul Magnuson, and Raimonda Modiano (London: Norton, 2004), p. 58. All subsequent page and line references are from this addition, abbreviated as '*AM 98*', and are given in parentheses after quotations in the text.
26 Samuel Taylor Coleridge, 'The Rime of the Ancient Mariner', in *Coleridge's Poetry and Prose,* ed. by Nicholas Halmi, Paul Magnuson, and Raimonda Modiano (London: Norton, 2004), p. 59. All subsequent page and line references are from this addition, abbreviated as '*AM 17*', and are given in parentheses after quotations in the text.
27 Marilyn Butler, *Romantics, Rebels and Reactionaries* (Oxford: Oxford University Press, 1981), p. 178.
28 Michael Levine, 'Pantheism', in *The Stanford Encyclopaedia of Philosophy* (Stanford University, 2012) http://plato.stanford.edu/entries/pantheism/ [accessed July 2024]
29 Samuel Taylor Coleridge, 'The Eolian Harp', in *Coleridge's Poetry and Prose*, ed. by Nicholas Halmi, Paul Magnuson, and Raimonda Modiano (London: Norton, 2004), ll. 39–41.
30 Samuel Taylor Coleridge, May 31st 1830, *Table Talk: Volume II*, ed. by Carl Woodring (London: Routledge, 1990), p. 249.
31 James Boulger, 'Christian Skepticism in The Ancient Mariner', in *From Sensibility to Romanticism*, ed. by Hilles and Bloom (Oxford: Oxford University Press, 1965), pp. 439–51 (p. 446).
32 James Chandler, *England in 1819* (Chicago: University of Chicago Press), pp. 42–3.
33 E. M. W. Tillyard, *Poetry and its Background* (London: Chatto & Windus, 1961), p. 80.

34 Marilyn Butler, *Romantics, Rebels and Reactionaries* (Oxford: Oxford University Press, 1981), p. 83.
35 Peter Kitson, 'Coleridge, the French Revolution, and "The Ancient Mariner": Collective Guilt and Individual Salvation', *The Yearbook of English Studies*, 19 (1989), 197–207 (207).
36 Nicholas Roe, *Wordsworth and Coleridge: The Radical Years* (Oxford: Oxford University Press, 1997), p. 38.
37 William Wordsworth, *The Prelude*, ed. by Ernest de Selincourt (Oxford: Oxford University Press, 1970), XIII. 264. All subsequent book and line references are from this addition, abbreviated as '*TP*', and are given in parentheses after quotations in the text.
38 Anon., 'Wordworth's Autobiographical Poem', *The Gentleman's Magazine,* 34: 188 (1850), 459–68 (466).
39 Alan Richardson, 'The Politics of Childhood: Wordsworth, Blake, and the Catechism Method', *ELH,* 56: 4 (1969), 853–68 (861–66).
40 David Duff, *Romanticism and the Uses of Genre* (Oxford: Oxford University Press, 2009), p. 90.
41 William Wordsworth, 'Essay Supplementary to the Preface', in *The Prose Works of William Wordsworth,* Vol. III, ed. by W. J. B. Owen and J. W. Smyser (Oxford: Clarendon Press, 1974), p. 63.
42 Richard Matlak, *Wordsworth's Trauma and Poetry: 1793–1803* (Milton: Routledge, 2024), p. 3.
43 Willard Spiegelman, *Wordsworth's Heroes* (Berkeley: University of California Press, 1985), pp. 127–29.
44 Nicholas Roe, 'Revising the Revolution: History and Imagination in *The Prelude*, 1799, 1805, 1850', in *Romantic Revisions*, ed. by Robert Brinkley and Keith Handley (Cambridge: Cambridge University Press, 1992), pp. 87–102 (p. 96).
45 William Wordsworth, 'Letter to the Bishops of Llandaff', in *The Prose Works of William Wordsworth,* ed. by W. J. B. Owen and Jane W. Smyser (Oxford: Clarendon Press, 1974), p. 52.
46 David Duff, *Romanticism and the Uses of Genre* (Oxford: Oxford University Press, 2009), p. 90.

# 2 Byron and Keats

## Intergenerational Conflict and Rising from the Fall

In the previous chapter I sought to demonstrate how the first-generation Romantics changed the way in which they defined their politics—and their roles as poets—in response to the French Revolution. In the case of Wordsworth and Coleridge this involved a fundamental change in their attitudes, abandoning their revolutionary and republican agendas in favour of a more conformist, conservative position. For these poets, the idea of the biblical Fall had a profound relevance to their experience of the failure of the French Revolution and its radical ideals. Their political transformation emerged from a sense that their misplaced pride and ambition had been chastened by failure in a way that echoed the Fall of Adam and Eve, and indeed that of Satan.

In the following chapter I shall argue that the second-generation Romantics—represented here by Byron and Keats—attempt to resurrect the radical ideologies abandoned by their predecessors. Referring principally to Byron's *Cain* (1821) and Keats's two unfinished versions of *Hyperion* (1818–1819), I will suggest that each of these poets uses the Miltonic idea of the necessary fall—that a good outcome can emerge from failure—to criticise the first generation's political malleability, and to make the case for ideological integrity. Both Byron and Keats were influenced and inspired to pursue a broadly libertarian, republican agenda by the early works of the first-generation Romantics, and in *Cain* and *Hyperion* we see their attempts to confront the fall of these high ideals in a post-revolutionary world.

### Byron: 'being/ Yourselves in your resistance'—The Value of Ideological Integrity in *Cain*

Byron's *Cain* is a play that is very much about intergenerational conflict, with the relationship between the play's eponymous protagonist and his parents being analogous, in my opinion, to the relationship between Byron and the first-generation Romantics. Byron identifies himself with the character of Cain in order to project an image of himself as a 'gloomy rebel, upholding truth, justice and freedom' in opposition to 'those who would submit in fear and self-abasement'.[1] In contrast to Cain's stoicism, Byron deliberately

DOI: 10.4324/9781003527466-4

frames the characters of Adam and Eve as timid and obsequious in the face of a repressive authority—an image which reflects Byron's view of the first-generation Romantics and their political transformation.

In this regard, *Cain* is typical of Byron's wider work, which is often 'directly concerned with the rebellion against traditional religious and social conventions', and thus implicates the first-generation Romantics as now belonging within that orthodox frame.[2] In *Cain*, Byron implicitly challenges the manner in which the first-generation Romantics used the idea of the necessary fall to justify their rejection of political radicalism and embrace a spirit of conventionality. By juxtaposing the images of the worn down, depleted figures of Adam and Eve with the fiery conviction of Cain, Byron's play illustrates that it is more honourable to hold to one's convictions, even at a severe cost, than to betray one's emotional and ideological instincts. In this sense, *Cain* disrupts the notion that an external event, such as the failure of the French Revolution, or indeed the biblical Fall itself, should alter an individual's principles.

For both Cain and Byron, the principal cause of conflict between themselves and their predecessors is the feeling that the second generation has been denied a birthright. In the case of Cain, he resents Adam and Eve for his family's ejection from Eden, an event which has condemned him to a life of hard labour and mortality:

> And this is
> Life. Toil! And wherefore should I toil? Because
> My father could not keep his place in Eden?
> What had I done in this? I was unborn;
> I sought not to be born; nor love the state
> To which that birth has brought me.[3]

This sense of having been robbed of a legacy also seems to reflect Byron's attitude towards the first-generation Romantics, although in his case it is a less literal form of Paradise from which he has been excluded. For Byron, it is the radical, egalitarian model of the state—the model which inspired the French Revolution—that he has been denied from participating in. To understand what I mean by this, it is useful to return to *The Prelude*. In that poem, Wordsworth describes the early, optimistic years of the French Revolution in terms which evoke an image of Europe not dissimilar to the Garden of Eden:

> Bliss was it in that dawn to be alive,
> But to be young was very Heaven!
> [...] Not favoured spots alone, but the whole Earth,
> The beauty wore of promise, that which sets,
> To take an image which was felt, no doubt,
> Among the bowers of Paradise itself,
> The budding rose above the rose full blown
>
> (*TP*, X. 693–706)

Although Byron was alive in the period that Wordsworth describes, he was so young that he may as well have been 'unborn'—he certainly had no opportunity to experience this 'bliss' first hand. Byron's only experience of this lost Paradise, like that of *Cain*, is in its aftermath. In Byron's long narrative poem, *Childe Harold's Pilgrimage* (1812), we see a stark example of the discrepancy between Wordsworth's and Byron's experiences of the revolution. In *The Prelude*, Wordsworth is able to recall a time when Europe appeared to have a positive vision for its future, whereas in *Childe Harold's Pilgrimage* Byron is only able to portray 'a Europe in ruins, wrecked by the violence unleashed by the French Revolution'.[4] For all intents and purposes, Byron's Europe is the same 'Land without Paradise' (*C*. I. 1) that Cain inhabits.

Of course, I am not seeking to suggest that Byron actually blamed the first-generation Romantics for the failure of the French Revolution itself—after all, none of the Romantic poets had any great political influence in 1790s France. The message which Byron uses *Cain* to convey is rather more subtle than this, though no less 'ideologically driven' or politically 'agitational'.[5] To understand this message, we must return once again to Cain's relationship with his parents.

When Cain confronts Adam about the Fall, he asks 'wherefore plucked ye not the tree of life?/ Ye might then have defied him' (*C*, I. 33–34). In truth, Cain knows that neither his father nor mother could have successfully challenged the 'all pow'rful' God (*C*, I. 76) any more than Wordsworth, say, could have changed the course of the French Revolution. What Cain resents his family for, then, is that in the face of their inevitable defeat they surrendered with meek resignation, betraying their true characters and principles in the process:

> [...] My father is
> Tamed down; my mother has forgot the mind
> Which made her thirst for knowledge at the risk
> Of an eternal curse
>
> (*C*, I. 179–182)

In this sense, Cain directly challenges the idea that his parents' fall was necessary in order to achieve a greater good. For him, Adam and Eve's argument that the biblical Fall was God's will, and therefore good, does not suffice. In his own words, Cain judges 'but by the fruits—and they are bitter' (*C*, I. 78).

It is exactly this kind of accusation which Byron seeks to level at the first-generation Romantics. In his satirical poem, *The Vision of Judgment* (1822), a direct reply to Robert Southey's *A Vision of Judgement* (1821), Byron explicitly accuses Southey of a weakness comparable to Adam and Eve's. He suggests that Southey has relinquished his true beliefs in the face of a hostile political environment, just as Adam and Eve surrender to God:

> He is—I will not say what—but I wish he was something else—I hate all intolerance—but most the intolerance of Apostasy—& the wretched vehemence with which a miserable creature who has contradicted himself—lies to his own heart—& endeavours to establish his sincerity by proving himself a rascal—*not* for changing his opinions—but for persecuting those who are of less malleable matter.[6]

The contradiction which Byron cites here refers to the publication of *Wat Tyler* (1817), a short play about the hero of a peasant revolt in the 1380s. The play, written by Southey in 1794, was belatedly discovered and published in 1817, causing Southey profound embarrassment. The play's overtly radical, republican message clashed with Southey's position as Poet Laureate, and his status as the 'ultra-ministerial *Quarterly Review*'s [...] most splenetic, reactionary critic'.[7] The incident perfectly captures the severity of the first-generation Romantics' political transformation and, for Byron, the extent of their betrayal of their true political instincts.

Extracts from *Wat Tyler* were read aloud in Parliament by William Smith MP, a member of the Whig opposition who wished to discredit the avowedly Tory Southey. In his response to Smith, in a letter of 1817, Southey gives his own justification for his apparently hypocritical stance. In it, he essentially puts forward the necessary fall argument—that he was an idealist in youth but that hard experience had given him a deeper wisdom:

> At that time and with those opinions, or rather feelings (for their root was in the heart and not in the understanding), I wrote *Wat Tyler* as one who was impatient of 'all the oppressions that are done under the sun'. The subject was injudiciously chosen, and it was treated as might be expected by a youth of twenty, in such times, who regarded only one side of the question.[8]

Southey's apparent dismissal of the heart in favour of the 'understanding' seems to bear out Byron's criticism that Southey 'lies to his own heart'. This is the key aspect of Byron's anger at the first-generation Romantics. He is not merely concerned that they had committed an act of hypocrisy, but that, like Adam and Eve, they had done so in spite of their emotional instincts.

In *Cain,* Byron appears to imply that the reason for this political and emotional inconsistency stems from fear. The play seems to suggest that Adam and Eve, and by extension the first-generation Romantics, abandon their principles out of fear of an authoritarian regime. In Adam and Eve's case, this authority is God himself. Indeed, Lucifer asserts that even the angels only praise God because they lack the bravery, or the moral conviction, to speak out against his autocratic 'tyranny':

They say what they must sing and say on pain
Of being that which I am and thou art —
[…] Souls who dare look the omnipotent tyrant in
His everlasting face and tell him that
His evil is not good!

(*C*, I. 134–140)

Paul Cantor suggests that by identifying God with the principle of evil here, Byron is seeking to 'justify revolution against established authority'.[9] While I agree with this interpretation, I believe that Byron goes further still, and that by making the omnipotent God a cruel authoritarian he is attempting to justify revolution against authority even when success is impossible—a twisted Kantian imperative to oppose tyranny, even when that tyrant is God himself. Indeed, Byron makes a similar suggestion in his ironic dedication to *Don Juan* (1819–1824). In the poem, Byron accuses Wordsworth, Coleridge, and Southey of abandoning their republicanism after the failure of the French Revolution because of their fear of state reprisals. Byron gives a Miltonic twist to this accusation by comparing the steadfastness of Milton's opposition to monarchy to the first-generation Romantics' betrayal of it:

He deigned not to belie his soul in songs,
Nor turn his very talent to a crime,
He did not loathe the sire, to laud the son,
But closed the tyrant-hater he begun.[10]

Byron is accusing the first generation of writing poetry purely to appease the establishment, just as the angels sing God's praises out of fear of retribution. In this sense, he undermines the first generation's characterisation of themselves as reformed characters. Whereas they would assert that the violence of the French Revolution had shown them the error of their political beliefs, Byron challenges them with the accusation that they are merely too weak to look their own 'omnipotent tyrant' in the face.

Of course, it could be suggested that Cain himself is not completely consistent in his defiance of God. Indeed, Wolf Hirst argues that Cain undergoes something of a necessary fall himself, suggesting that Cain, 'Spiritually blinded by pride, […] causes the death of a close relative, and then gains moral knowledge and self recognition'.[11] However, I would assert that Hirst misinterprets *Cain*'s ending. He implies that the murder of Abel leads Cain to give up his rebellious feelings, and to accept that God is not the tyrant that Cain had once believed. But Cain does no such thing. Certainly, Cain regrets the death of his brother and repeatedly curses himself for it, but he never offers to renounce the principles which caused him to rebel in the first place. Indeed, when God's Angel comes to admonish Cain, Cain defends himself by saying: 'I did not seek/ For life nor did I make myself' (*C*, III. 509–510), echoing his complaint at the beginning of the play that he had no part in the Original Sin. His central grievance—that God is ultimately responsible for mankind's suffering—has not changed. In this sense, we may see the death of Abel as analogous with the violence of the French Revolution. Both are regrettable consequences of the rebellion against tyranny—falls in their own right—but they do not, to Byron at least, invalidate the principles upon which that rebellion was founded.

*Cain*, then, is a play that wholeheartedly rejects the idea of the necessary fall, and instead promotes ideological integrity as a paramount virtue. It is the failure to adhere to their beliefs which prompts his resentment of the first-generation Romantics—a resentment which we see reflected in Cain's relationship with his parents. For Byron, the idea that an external event, however powerful, should change one's most deeply held convictions is a form of moral and ideological cowardice. In *Cain*, Byron presents us with the ultimate story of a man who will not lay aside his beliefs, even in the face of a vengeful God, and who is prepared to accept the consequences of failure.

In the next section of this chapter we will encounter another example of how the 'second-generation Romantics deployments of myth have consistently political and polemical [...] functions'.[12]

## Keats: The Necessary Transition to a New Poetic Order

Like *Cain*, Keats's *Hyperion: A Fragment* (1819) and *The Fall of Hyperion: A Dream* (1820) are poems which concern the idea of poetic identity, as well as the more immediate political and poetic contexts of the time. After Keats's death, Byron himself acknowledged the redolence of *Hyperion* with his own work and ideas, singling it out for praise: 'I did not approve of Keats's poetry, or principles of poetry', he wrote, yet added that '*Hyperion* is a fine monument, and will keep his name'.[13] Nicholas Roe suggests that Byron's begrudging praise of Keats arises from an 'uneasy sense of self-recognition in Keats's poetic manner'.[14] What I will suggest here is that what Byron recognised in the *Hyperion* poems was a similar manoeuvring against the position of the first-generation Romantics that we find in *Cain*, as well as an application of the same Miltonic ideas which anchor Byron's play.

The nature of Keats's opposition to the first-generation Romantics is not identical to Byron's. Whereas Byron deplores the inconsistency, or even duplicity, of the first-generation Romantics, Keats is far more open to ideas of change and duality. Indeed, the *Hyperion* poems themselves are explicitly about change, or more accurately transition. Like *Paradise Lost*—of which both pieces form 'a comprehensive reinterpretation in the light of [Keats's] own thinking and experience'—the poems are about a fall.[15] In the case of *Hyperion* this fall concerns the Grecian Titans but, just as in Milton's work, these poems are also about the rise of something new: the Olympian gods. I believe that this is Keats's way of addressing his role as part of the new wave of poets that we now recognise as the second-generation Romantics. The rise of the Olympians mirrors Keats's own ideas about the shifting political and poetic landscape of post-Waterloo England. In the same way that the youthful Apollo arises to challenge Hyperion, Keats perceives himself as being among the natural successors to figures such as Wordsworth and Coleridge. What I shall argue here, therefore, is that the *Hyperion* poems present a generational version of the necessary fall—a poetic 'dramatization of the warring stances which [Keats] adopts toward poetic autonomy and the literary past', which states the case for the passing of an old generation of poets to make way for a new one.[16] It is a necessary fall in order to fulfil a necessary transition.

At this point we must return to Harold Bloom. I wrote in the Preface to this book that his ideas of poetic heredity are not universally accepted, but one cannot deny their relevance when discussing Keats and *Hyperion*. In the introduction to his celebrated book, *The Anxiety of Influence*, Bloom frames the argument that the progress of the poetic tradition rests on a sense of anxiety, suggesting that each generation of poets is anxious not only to match the efforts of their esteemed predecessors, but to exceed them and attain a position of 'priority'. Bloom couches this argument in Freudian terms, posing the struggle between poetic generations as not unlike that between the mythic archetypes of father and son, Laius and Oedipus, with each fresh generation feeling the pressure of their 'father's' influence and seeking to overthrow them. In poetic terms, this weight of anxiety stems from a sense of inferiority that can only be vanquished by eclipsing the 'father' poet's literary achievements.[17]

Of course, looking back to the previous section we can find this sense of familial tension in *Cain*, and yet I would resist the notion that Byron is expressing anything that one could meaningfully interpret as poetic anxiety. His respect for Milton is clear in his choice of model for his play, but the freedom with which he toys with his source material engenders more a sense of playful confidence than anxiety. Meanwhile, his implicit contempt for the first-generation Romantics is rooted in politics and seems to brook no real sense of concern with defeating their poetic position. Keats, however, is a different case.

When one begins to look for the sense of necessary poetic transition in the *Hyperion* poems, one thing is striking. The very fact that there are two versions of the poem—*Hyperion: A Fragment* and *The Fall of Hyperion: A Dream*—immediately implies a sense of poetic transition and development. In a letter to his friend and fellow writer, John Hamilton Reynolds, Keats claimed that he had abandoned the first version of the poem because it was too 'Miltonic':

> I have given up on *Hyperion* — there were too many Miltonic inversions in it—Miltonic verse cannot be written but in an artful or rather artist's humour. I wish to give myself up to other sensations.[18]

Keats's aversion here to being too 'artful' seems to tie in to his desire to differentiate himself from what has gone before—in this case Milton—in a manner that underlines Bloom's theory of the struggle against 'influence'. In the same letter to Reynolds, Keats expresses a desire to move away from the 'false beauty proceeding from art, and [...] to the true voice of feeling'.[19] For Keats, the aborted first attempt at *Hyperion* produces an unmistakeable feeling of anxiety—a fear that his work resembles too closely the work of his poetic ancestor, rather than being something truly original emerging from within his own mind and feelings.

It is certainly the case that the first *Hyperion* poem is less 'original' than *The Fall*. In terms of structure and theme, *Hyperion* directly mirrors much of *Paradise Lost*. For example, the poem begins with the Titans after their own fall, in much the same way that Milton's poem begins with Satan and the rebellious angels in Hell. In addition, the birth of Apollo in Delos, a natural paradise, invites a direct comparison to the creation of Adam and Eve. In moving away from these more overtly Miltonic narrative structures in *The Fall*, Stuart M. Sperry Jr argues that Keats reaches 'for a form that is both more personal and allegoric', adding that this 'change is sweeping, involving not only the structure but the style'.[20] Although *Hyperion* operates on a much deeper level than a mere parody of Milton—as I shall go on to demonstrate—when one compares it to *The Fall*, it is understandable that Keats should characterise his first attempt as being too superficial to meet his ambitions. In this sense, Keats's failure to complete *Hyperion* is a necessary transition of its own—a failure which leads him to reassess his poetic identity and to articulate these reflections in *The Fall*.

The most significant change between the two poems, for the purposes of this discussion, is the manner in which *The Fall* shifts the emphasis of its theme towards poetry and the role of the poet, making this the overt driving force of the narrative. *The Fall* begins with a first-person narrator and poet figure who, having fallen into a dream state, is confronted by the last of the Titans, Moneta. In this meeting the poet is challenged to ascend a dais where he is confronted about the nature of poets and poetry, as well as being shown visions of Hyperion in his palace, as well as the fallen Titans below. As Sperry puts it:

> It is clear from the logic and structure of Keats's narrative that the altar toward which the dreamer advances represents the higher condition he must achieve in rising from mere visionary to poet.[21]

Through this use of a humanised, striving poet figure in place of the innately godly Apollo, Keats is better able to create the sense of personal originality that he felt was lacking in *Hyperion*. Indeed, shorn of its more overtly Miltonic architecture, *The Fall* becomes, in the words of John D. Rosenburg, 'less an epic than a personal statement'—a poem absolutely rooted in Keats's individual poetic sensibility.[22]

However, despite all of the differences between the two versions of *Hyperion*, and the fact that they remained unfinished, the underlying message which I believe Keats sought to convey remains largely the same in each poem. Keats's principal aim in the *Hyperion* poems is to distinguish between two different ways of approaching poetry, and between the two poetic generations of his era. This comparison is most acutely drawn in the contrast between Hyperion and Apollo, a comparison which translates across both versions of the poem.

Before delving into the function of these two characters in the *Hyperion* poems themselves, though, it is important to observe that Keats had a long-standing fascination with the figure of Apollo. Throughout his work, Keats often associates Apollo with the purest essence of poetry. In 1817, for instance, the year before Keats began composing *Hyperion*, he wrote 'Ode to Apollo' (1817). In the 'Ode', Keats gives a condensed account of the greatest poets in history, where he suggests that all of their achievements stem from the poetic influence of this 'God of Bards'.[23] When we turn to the *Hyperion* poems, therefore, we must be cognisant of the full significance of Hyperion's position as Apollo's rival. In effect, by opposing Apollo, Hyperion opposes the true spirit of poetry.

This division between Hyperion and Apollo is especially significant because Keats seeks to present the relationship as directly analogous with the relationship between the first- and second-generation Romantics. Indeed, Richard Cronin suggests that the parallel may be even more intimate than this, and that Keats is in fact seeking to identify himself personally with the figure of Apollo:

> The plot of *Hyperion,* in which Saturn and the Titans are ousted, and Hyperion is forced to recognise the nobler music of Apollo, seems designed to express Keats's heady sense of his own irresistible genius.[24]

Cronin's suggestion here is compelling, especially when one considers the way in which Keats uses images of wealth to differentiate between Apollo and Hyperion. As a 'Cockney poet', Keats was famously ridiculed by the elite literary establishment for his relatively modest background. Christopher Rovee usefully provides a list of some of the various terms of abuse levelled at Keats in his short career: 'trash, unclean, secondhand, vulgar, polluter, disgusting, wasteful'—a raft of terms which are deliberately used to associate Keats with the 'grime of London', and mock his supposed lack of a classical education.[25] It is interesting, therefore, to note the disparities between the description of Hyperion's home in *The Fall* and Delos, the birthplace of Apollo, as described in *Hyperion*. Hyperion's palace is outwardly a glorious 'palace bright,/ Bastioned with pyramids of glowing gold', and yet 'Instead of sweets, his [Hyperion's] ample palate takes/ Savour of poisonous brass and metal stick'.[26] In comparison, Delos is described in terms of natural beauty, without the implied sense of an underlying malaise: 'Rejoice, O Delos, with thine olives green,/ and poplars, and lawn-shading palms, and beech'.[27]

The implication here, that Apollo's island represents a more authentic kind of beauty, is reinforced by Apollo's named status as the 'Father of all verse' (*H*, III. 13). Not only does this identify Apollo and his environs with the genuine essence of poetry, but also implies a sense that wealth or high position can undermine poetic sensibilities. In my opinion, this is a direct expression of Keats's view of his own position in relation to his poetic predecessors. Although the likes of Southey and Wordsworth could not necessarily be described as wealthy, their acceptance of grandiose titles and institutional roles and payouts, such as Southey's Poet Laureateship, stand in stark contrast to Keats's conferred epithet of 'Mr John' the apothecary.[28]

It is possible, however, to extend the thematic significance of wealth in the *Hyperion* poems even further than mere poetic rivalry. Marilyn Butler points out that the overthrow of the wealthy and powerful Titans appears to be as much an allegory about the French Revolution as it is about poetry:

> *Hyperion* does after all describe a revolution, the overthrow of the Titans by the Olympian gods. Its main literary source, *Paradise Lost*, is about the father of all rebellions, Satan's. There is evidence in the letters that Keats [...] had become interested in the French Revolution.[29]

It is certainly the case that Keats empathised with the struggle against entitlement. Many critics, notably Nicholas Roe, have done much to historicise and politicise Keats's poetry. In Roe's view, the 'successive acts of usurpation' in *Hyperion*—the overthrow of the Titans by the Olympian Gods—reflects Keats's view of political history as a series of peaks and troughs or, as I would call them, necessary transitions.[30] However, that the *Hyperion* poems are explicitly about the French Revolution is a difficult interpretation to sustain. The sincere pathos with which Keats treats the fallen Titans seems too heartfelt, too empathetic to suggest a link with the overthrown aristocrats of France. The description of Thea as an admixture of extreme loveliness and grief, 'How beautiful, if sorrow had not made/ Sorrow more beautiful than Beauty's self' (*H*, I. 34–35), does nothing to evoke the vehemence of Keats's opposition to monarchs and aristocracy. In an annotation to his copy of *Paradise Lost,* Keats wrote of Satan's ire towards God's apparent tyranny, 'How noble and collected an indignation against Kings'.[31] It does not seem credible, then, that Keats would invest any sympathy onto the deposed despots of France if he was unwilling to lend any to God himself.

And yet, it would be unwise to discount the obvious revolutionary themes of the *Hyperion* poems. As I have already intimated, the revolution Keats is really seeking to grapple with is a poetic one. The Titans may not resemble the fallen nobility of France, but in a set of poems so overtly about poets, and the role and value of poetry, it seems entirely plausible that they should represent the politically 'fallen' poets of the previous generation. Certainly, that would fit the pattern of poetic usurpation set by Apollo, while also explaining Keats's empathetic style. After all, Keats had admired the first-generation Romantics enormously, openly acclaiming Wordsworth as a 'genius'.[32] His disappointment in their turn away from radicalism would be, therefore, like his description of Thea, tinged with poignant sadness. Writing about Wordsworth in a letter to his brother, Keats decried the older poet's 'egotism, Vanity, and bigotry', but qualified his insult by adding that 'he is a great poet if not a philosopher'.[33] Keats, it seems, was characteristically anxious; torn between admiration and his own feelings of moral and poetic superiority. In this sense, the French Revolution not only occasioned a disruption in the political hierarchies of Europe, but also, in the eyes of Keats, the poetic hierarchies as well. The fact that the *Hyperion* poems remain unfinished may represent Keats's difficulty in establishing his proper place in this new order—his difficulty in completing the necessary transition to his own place among the great poets, and his usurpation of the previous generation.

In this sense, the fact that both of the *Hyperion* poems remain incomplete could make my central argument problematic, perhaps suggesting an unwillingness on Keats's part to dethrone his former idols. Jonathan Bate, however, provides us with a potential answer, citing how Keats's idea of negative capability provides evidence that *The Fall* 'had to remain a fragment like the poem it was revising', and that in its 'lack of closure *Hyperion* had found its true form'.[34] Keats only ever explains negative capability once, in a letter to his brothers in 1817—the year before he began *Hyperion*—but it has had a profound impact on the way in which critics like Bate have read Keats:

> Negative Capability, that is, when a man is capable of being in uncertainties, mysteries, doubts, without any irritable reaching after fact and reason—Coleridge, for instance, would let go by a fine isolated verisimilitude caught from the Penetralium of mystery, from being incapable of remaining content with half-knowledge. This pursued through volumes would perhaps take us no further than this, that with a great poet the sense of Beauty overcomes every other consideration, or rather obliterates all consideration.[35]

Keats's assertion—that beauty in itself should be the primary concern of poets and poetry—is vital in helping us to interpret Keats's understanding of his own role in a new generation of poets. His specific criticism of Coleridge, one of the foremost first-generation Romantics, is that he is incapable of being 'content' with beauty on its own, and always requires a complete and rationalised meaning to his philosophy, and perhaps his poetry also. That Keats did not finish either version of *Hyperion*, therefore, is a powerful statement in itself. Their incompleteness defies Coleridge's 'irritable reaching after fact and reason' and embodies Keats's 'willingness to live with uncertainties and doubts'.[36] As Christoph Bode argues, '*The Fall of Hyperion* is a *necessary* fragment' because its very truncation is a statement in itself. A statement 'that could not possibly have been surpassed by a continuation of the tale. The *Fall of Hyperion* is complete'.[37] Thus, the fragmentary nature of Keats's poems becomes a powerful challenge to the first-generation Romantics, perpetuating rather than undermining the necessary transition to a new poetic order.

As I suggested at the beginning of this section, it is indeed intergenerational conflict which drives the narrative of the *Hyperion* poems. What I have sought to demonstrate here is the way in which Keats seeks to undermine his predecessors' poetic credentials while promoting his own. His deliberate effort to align himself with the figure of Apollo signals his desire to emerge from his comparatively humble origins and to challenge the established pecking order. Like Byron's *Cain*, the *Hyperion* poems are overtly Miltonic, borrowing elements of both plot and theme from *Paradise Lost*, but just as with *Cain*, *Hyperion* reinvents its genesis. Whereas *Paradise Lost* is a story about a misguided, though ultimately necessary rebellion, Keats's poems assert a positive case for change: a necessary transition.

The focus on intergenerational conflict/transition that we find in *Cain* and *Hyperion* is a recurrent theme throughout the work of what we now call the second-generation Romantics. This is perhaps reflective of the premature deaths of this grouping's most famous members: Byron, Keats, and Percy Shelley. Because they never fully matured as poets, their writing is necessarily bound up with a sense of their youth—a feeling of philosophical exuberance and emerging ideological perspectives that provokes a contrast with the increasing conservatism of their older contemporaries.

In addition, the social and historical context of the late 1810s and early 1820s seems to invite the narrative of change that we find in the work of these young poets. The defeat of Napoleon at Waterloo in 1815, accompanied by an increasingly turbulent atmosphere in domestic politics—demonstrated most disturbingly by the Peterloo Massacre of 1819—all contribute to creating a transitory atmosphere in this period. William Hazlitt, for instance, writing in 1824 in *The Spirit of the Age*, expressed his sense of witnessing the end of a political and cultural era. In the book, which Paul Schlicke describes as a 'largely melancholy and entirely retrospective' piece, Hazlitt bemoans the 'ineffectual chattering of Samuel Taylor Coleridge', as well as the 'egoism of Wordsworth', citing them as evidence of the ultimate failure of the idealistic spirit that had inspired the French Revolution which, for Hazlitt, had characterised the era between the 1790s and 1820s.[38]

For younger writers, like Byron and Percy Shelley, however, this seemingly pivotal shift in the nature of society was not necessarily perceived with quite the same cynicism as Hazlitt. Indeed, one might suggest that it presented to their imagination a feeling of opportunity—a chance to revive, rather than say farewell to, a spirit of adventurous radicalism. If one looks, for example, at Percy Bysshe Shelley's *A Philosophical View of Reform* (1820)—his response to the increasingly repressive measures of the government—it exudes a defiant and radical spirit. The treatise includes a list of bold propositions, including the disbandment of the standing army, the equality of all religions under the law, the abolition of corrupt offices and sinecures, as well as asserting the 'necessity of a material change' in the institutions and power structures of the country more generally.[39] There is certainly little sense of cynicism or lack of ambition.

And yet, ultimately, these grand proposals would not come to pass, or at least not in the manner or pace that Shelley might have envisaged. A failure that neither he, Byron, or Keats would live to witness. Indeed, their deaths may well have contributed to Hazlitt's feelings of pessimism for the future. In Part II of this book, I will explore how the literature of this new, post-Romantic era developed. Beginning with a survivor of that generation of writers, Mary Shelley, I will focus particularly on her prescient scepticism about the future of Percy Shelley's optimistic vision for the future, and the trajectory of radical politics as he and his circle imagined it. I will then move on to examine more widely how the literature of the late 1810s and early 1820s reflects a growing feeling of destabilisation, and a concern about the disruption of established patterns of cultural and political identity. As in the previous chapters, I shall seek to explore all this through the prism of Miltonic ideas of the Fall.

## Notes

1 David Eggenschweiller, 'Byron's *Cain* and the Antimythological Myth', in *The Plays of Lord Byron: Critical Essays*, ed. by Robert Gleckner and Bernard Beatty (Liverpool: Liverpool University Press, 1997), p. 235.
2 Edward E. Bostetter, 'Byron and the Politics of Paradise', *PMLA*, 75: 5 (1960), 571–76 (571).
3 George Gordon Byron, *Lord Byron's Cain*, ed. by T. G. Steffan (Austin: University of Texas, 1968), X. 693–706. All subsequent line references are from this edition, abbreviated as '*C*', and are given in parentheses after quotations in the text.
4 Paul Cantor, 'The Politics of the Epic: Wordsworth, Byron, and the Romantic Redefinition of Heroism', *The Review of Politics*, 69: 3 (2007), 375–401 (393).
5 Peter A. Schock, 'The "Satanism" of Cain in Context: Byron's Lucifer and the War against Blasphemy', *Keats-Shelley Journal*, 44 (1995), 182–215 (214).
6 Byron, *The Vision of Judgement*, ed. by Mary Redman (Cambridge: Cambridge University Press, 1926), p. 4.
7 Charles Mahoney, *Romantics and Renegades: The Poetics of Political Reaction* (Basingstoke: Palgrave Macmillan, 2002), p. 125.
8 Robert Southey, 'Letter to William Smith MP, 1817', in *The Life and Correspondence of Robert Southey*, ed. by Charles Cuthbert Southey (London: Longman, Brown, Green, and Longmans, 1849), p. 376, https://lordbyron.org/contents.php?doc=RoSouth.1849.Contents [accessed July 2024]

9 Paul Cantor, 'Byron's *Cain*: A Romantic Version of the Fall', *The Kenyon Review*, 2: 3 (1980), 50–71 (55).
10 Byron, *Don Juan* (Harmondsworth: Penguin, 1977), p. 4.
11 Wolf Z. Hirst, 'Byron's Lapse into Orthodoxy: An Unorthodox Reading of Cain', in *The Plays of Lord Byron: Critical Essays*, ed. by Robert Gleckner and Bernard Beatty (Liverpool: Liverpool University Press, 1997), p. 254.
12 Peter A. Schock, 'The "Satanism" of Cain in Context: Byron's Lucifer and the War against Blasphemy', *Keats-Shelley Journal*, 44 (1995), 182–215 (184).
13 George Gordon Byron, 'Letter to John Murray, July 30th 1821', in *Byron A Self-Portrait Letters and Diaries, Vol II*, ed. by Peter Quennell (London: John Murray, 1950), p. 661.
14 Nicholas Roe, *John Keats and the Culture of Dissent* (Oxford: Clarendon Press, 1997), p. 18.
15 Stuart M. Sperry Jr, 'Keats, Milton, and the Fall of Hyperion', *PMLA*, 77: 1 (1962), 77–84 (78).
16 Carl Plasa, 'Revision and Repression in Keats's Hyperion: "Pure Creations of the Poet's Brain"', *Keats-Shelley Journal*, 44 (1995), 117–46 (125).
17 Harold Bloom, *The Anxiety of Influence* (Oxford: Oxford University Press, 1997), pp. 5–16.
18 John Keats, 'Letter to John Hamilton Reynolds', 21 September 1819, in *The Letters of John Keats,* ed. by Maurice Forman (Oxford: Oxford University Press, 1952), p. 384.
19 John Keats, 'Letter to John Hamilton Reynolds', 21 September 1819, in *The Letters of John Keats,* ed. by Maurice Forman (Oxford: Oxford University Press, 1952), p. 384.
20 Stuart M. Sperry Jr, 'Keats, Milton, and the Fall of Hyperion', *PMLA*, 77: 1 (1962), 77–84 (77).
21 Stuart M. Sperry Jr, 'Keats, Milton, and the Fall of Hyperion', *PMLA*, 77: 1 (1962), 77–84 (78).
22 John D. Rosenberg, 'Keats and Milton: The Paradox of Rejection', *Keats-Shelley Journal*, 6 (1957), 87–95 (91).
23 Keats, 'Ode to Apollo', in *Keats's Poetry and Prose*, ed. by Jeffrey Cox (London: Norton, 2009), l. 47.
24 Richard Cronin, 'Keats and the Politics of Cockney Style', *Studies in English Literature, 1500–1900*, 36: 4 (1996), 785–806 (796).
25 Christopher Rovee, 'Trashing Keats', *EHL*, 75: 4 (2008), 993–1022 (993).
26 John Keats, 'The Fall of Hyperion: A Dream', in *Keats's Poetry and Prose*, ed. by Jeffrey Cox (London: Norton, 2009), II. 24–33. All subsequent line references are from the same edition, abbreviated as '*TF*', and are given in parenthesis after quotations in the text.
27 John Keats, 'Hyperion: A Fragment', in *Keats's Poetry and Prose*, ed. by Jeffrey Cox (London: Norton, 2009), III. 2–25. All subsequent line references are from the same edition, abbreviated as '*H*', and are given in parenthesis after quotations in the text.
28 J. G. Lockhart, 'Review of *Endymion*: The Cockney School of Poetry IV', *Blackwood's Edinburgh Magazine*, 3 (1818), in *Keats's Poetry and Prose*, ed. by Jeffrey Cox (London: Norton, 2009), p. 273.
29 Marilyn Butler, *Romantics, Rebels and Reactionaries* (Oxford: Oxford University Press, 1981), p. 151.
30 Nicholas Roe, *John Keats and the Culture of Dissent* (Oxford: Clarendon Press, 1997), p. 57.
31 Keats, quoted by John Barnard, *John Keats* (Cambridge: Cambridge University Press, 1987), p. 58.

32 Keats, 'Letter to John Reynolds May 3rd 1818', in *Keats's Poetry and Prose*, ed. by Jeffrey Cox (London: Norton, 2009), p. 243.
33 Keats, 'Letter to George and Thomas Keats', 27 February 1818, in *The Letters of John Keats,* ed. by Maurice Forman (Oxford: Oxford University Press, 1952), p. 106.
34 Jonathan Bate, 'Keats's Two Hyperions and the Problem of Milton', in *Romantic Revisions*, ed. by Robert Brinkley and Keith Handley (Cambridge: Cambridge University Press, 1992), pp. 321–38 (p. 337).
35 Keats, 'Letter to George and Thomas Keats', 21 December 1817, in *The Letters of John Keats,* ed. by Maurice Forman (Oxford: Oxford University Press, 1952), p. 71.
36 Jonathan Bate, 'Keats's Two Hyperions and the Problem of Milton', in *Romantic Revisions*, ed. by Robert Brinkley and Keith Handley (Cambridge: Cambridge University Press, 1992), pp. 321–38 (p. 336).
37 Christoph Bode, 'Hyperion, "The Fall of Hyperion", and Keats's Poetics', *The Wordsworth Circle*, 31: 1 (2000), 31–7 (31–2).
38 Paul Schlicke, 'Hazlitt, Horne and the Spirit of the Age', *Studies in English Literature*, 45: 4 (2005), 829–51 (829).
39 Percy Bysshe Shelley, *A Philosophical View of Reform*, ed. by T. W. Rolleston (Oxford: Oxford University Press, 1920), p. 1.

# Part II

# Writing from the Literary 'Lacuna'

## Divided Voices and Divided Sympathies

In *Romantic Victorians* (2002), Richard Cronin suggests that the years between 1824 and 1840 'do not constitute a literary period at all, but something more in the way of a lacuna, a dash, or some other kind of punctuation mark'.[1] Certainly, with the premature deaths of some of its most significant figureheads, such as Byron in 1824, there is a sense that the Romantic period ended before its time, and with the coronation of Queen Victoria not taking place until 1837, one cannot comfortably label literature composed in the years which preceded it as Victorian. This ambiguous period is also one of political and social transition, in which firm groupings and labels are difficult to maintain. In 1832, a reviewer for *Tait's Edinburgh Magazine* attempted to express this sense of upheaval:

> A change has come over the spirit of the Time; mighty questions have been stirred; deep interests have been created; vast masses of men, formerly inert and impassive, have begun to heave to and fro with the force of a newly inspired animation; old things are passing away—all things are becoming new.[2]

This period, then, should not be mistaken for a mere historical blip, but rather, as Cronin suggests, an under-explored moment of historical change. Cronin's description of the period as a 'lacuna', although capturing this sense of transition, belies the intense confusion, pain, and excitement that those living in this time experienced. Major events such as the Reform Act of 1832, which fundamentally restructured the electoral system, or the ongoing acceleration of industrialisation and urbanisation, which dramatically changed the way in which people lived and worked, all took place in this 'punctuation mark' of literary history.

In Part II of this book, I will give particular attention to the way in which the literature of this 'lacuna' period makes use of divided narrative voices and divided characters, modelled upon the divided poet figure of *Paradise Lost*,

DOI: 10.4324/9781003527466-5

to reflect the sense of strife and conflict in this transitory historical moment. Referring principally to Mary Shelley's *Frankenstein* (1818) and James Hogg's *Confessions of a Justified Sinner* (1824), before moving forward to Emily Brontë's *Wuthering Heights* (1847), I seek to explore how the writers of this period interpret the decline of a set of particular cultural and political ideas, which we may today refer to as Romantic, or indeed radical. I shall describe how the divisions within these novels express an awareness that one coherent era has drawn to a close, and that a new one has yet to establish itself. I shall also argue that Cronin's defined boundaries of 1824 and 1840 can, and should, be extended to accommodate texts like the ones I have chosen here—texts which fall either side of his proposed lacuna, but do not comfortably conform to either a Romantic or Victorian template.

These specific texts not only provide a chronological pathway between Romanticism and Victorianism, but also share particular qualities with each other. Most significantly for this project, the Miltonic ideas of the Fall which I described in the Introduction and throughout Part I have a strong and peculiar relevance to each of these novels. Also, the use of divided, conflicting voices which we find in *Paradise Lost*, seen vividly in the contrast between Satan and the poem's epic narrator, are a major characteristic of the novels I will be discussing here.

## Notes

1 Richard Cronin, *Romantic Victorians* (Basingstoke: Palgrave, 2002), p. 2.
2 *Tait's Edinburgh Review* (April, 1832), quoted by Ian Duncan, *Scott's Shadow* (Princeton: Princeton University Press, 2007), p. 301.

# 3 *Frankenstein* and Mary Shelley's Radical Scepticism

*Frankenstein* owes much to *Paradise Lost*: the novel's characters, plot, and themes all have some connection with the poem. Indeed, the epigraph to the novel itself is taken from it: 'Did I request thee, Maker, from/ My clay to mould me Man?/ Did I solicit thee from darkness to promote me'.[1] Sandra M. Gilbert and Susan Gubar have written to great effect about Shelley as one of 'Milton's daughters', and regard *Frankenstein* as a rewriting of *Paradise Lost*, using its structures and themes to deliver a work that is simultaneously homage and critique.[2] It is certainly the case that *Frankenstein* is concerned with the Miltonic ideas of the Fall that this book focuses on, most especially the division of narrative voices and roles, as well as wider questions about the nature of fallenness. However, rather than seeking to offer justifications for the ways of God (or indeed poets), Mary Shelley uses these Miltonic devices to express an uneasy sense that the radical, male-dominated politics of the Romantic period—a politics she was intensely drawn to—were not completely equipped to deal with the problems of the post-revolutionary, post-Napoleonic period in which she found herself. Far from being a work concerned with justifying itself, it is a novel that ultimately seeks to question and interrogate the political and moral justifications of others.

To understand the political implications of *Frankenstein*, it is worth considering the circumstances of its composition. The story is well known and is recounted in the preface to the novel. In the summer of 1816, Byron, Percy Shelley, John Polidori, and Mary Shelley—then Mary Godwin—were telling ghost stories at Lake Geneva. Before the game was complete, however, her companions left her to go for an expedition in the nearby Alps. Afterwards, she continued her work alone until it became the novel we now recognise.[3] This story is significant, not only because it provides the geographical backdrop for *Frankenstein*, but because it also hints at a subtle, but important and growing, division between Mary and her companions—a personal and political division which, once recognised, can be said to define the novel.

At just 19 years of age in 1816, Mary was the junior member of a radical movement of thinkers and writers of which her parents, William Godwin and her then-deceased mother Mary Wollstonecraft, could be considered

DOI: 10.4324/9781003527466-6

pioneers—with Percy Shelley and Lord Byron as its most high-profile contemporary figureheads. And yet, despite being the youngster of this group, Mary Shelley was not afraid to interrogate and engage with the principles upon which this radical circle was based, especially as it related to her estranged father. Indeed, as Beth Lau notes, the novel's conflicted treatment of father figures, along with the ideas and positions associated with Godwin and his circle, can easily be read as a reflection of Mary Shelley's 'notoriously complex relationship with her own father'.[4]

For instance, the 'Godwinian' idea that knowledge and its pursuit are an absolute good for society comes under severe scrutiny in *Frankenstein.* The novel's two central narratives—those of Captain Walton and Victor Frankenstein—both concern the danger of placing the quest for knowledge and the resulting betterment of mankind above the more direct responsibilities to one's friends and family. Walton, in his efforts to reach the North Pole, almost kills his entire crew, while Frankenstein's experiments lead to the deaths of almost everyone he loves. The moral virtue of focusing on the wider good is always stressed by Godwin, who deems it every person's responsibility to 'contribute, so far as it lies in their power, to the pleasure and benefit of each other'.[5] However, that this very philosophy leads to such profound discord in their personal lives, most dramatically in the case of Frankenstein himself, surely carries with it a profound 'biographic resonance'.[6]

The examples of Walton and Frankenstein are best interpreted as a vision of what can go wrong when one becomes obsessed with any kind of ideology, but especially when that ideology's stated purpose is the betterment of mankind. Frankenstein's speech to Walton at the end of the novel provides a perfect summation of this point, as he recalls how his lofty intention of creating an ideal human, free of sin and corruption, proved to be beyond what he had believed himself capable of:

> When younger [...] I felt as if I were destined for some great enterprise. My feelings are profound; but I possessed a coolness of judgement that fitted me for illustrious achievements. This sentiment of the worth of my nature supported me, when others would have been oppressed; for I deemed it criminal to throw away in useless grief those talents that might be useful to my fellow creatures [...] But this feeling, which supported me in the commencement of my career, now only serves to plunge me lower in the dust.
>
> (*F*, p. 186)

What Shelley seems to be questioning here is how far one should go for the attainment of any ambition, even when the ambition is an admirable one. In so doing, she also offers an oblique criticism of both her father's and her lover's commitment to their radical philosophy.

Jane Blumberg puts the point well, describing *Frankenstein* as a novel which, although 'undeniably constructed out of the currency of the radical movement', is also a 'critique of that system and of the personalities of the men who were its proponents'.[7] Returning again to Mary Shelley's personal history, it is not difficult to find examples of ambitious, radical, and well-intentioned men bringing disaster down on their loved ones. Percy Shelley's failure to support her financially during her first pregnancy, a situation aggravated by her father's demands for money from Shelley, all point to a character weakness in the men for whom Mary Shelley cared—a particularly 'macho' heedlessness of consequences which is at the very core of *Frankenstein.* Irene Taylor and Gina Luria capture this dynamic when they write that the novel can be read as 'Romantic Woman's ultimate judgement of the alienated artist of male romanticism'.[8] The story of the novel's conception—Byron and Percy Shelley walking off into the mountains while leaving Mary behind—takes on a new dimension when examined from this perspective. She was not always prepared to follow them.

In this respect, the divided narratives of Walton and Frankenstein give us an insight into Shelley's views on the limits and dangers of obsessive ambition and idealism. The most illustrative example of this can be found when Walton's ship is trapped by ice and his crew urge him to return south if they are freed rather than continue with his expedition to the North Pole. At this point, the voices of the two narrators—Walton and Frankenstein—overlap, as the latter gives an impassioned rebuke to the crew:

> Are you then so easily turned from your design? [...] You were hereafter to be hailed as the benefactors of your species; your name adored, as belonging to brave men who encountered death for honour and the benefit of mankind [...] Do not return to your families with the stigma of disgrace marked on your brows.
>
> (*F*, p. 190)

This passage occurs in one of the last of Walton's letters home to his sister. In the next two letters, although he curses the 'cowardice' and 'indecision' (*F*, p. 191) of himself and his crew, Walton reveals that he has consented to turn south if they should be freed from the ice. On hearing the news, Frankenstein reasserts his intention to continue with his quest, despite Walton's capitulation: 'You may give up on your purpose; but mine is assigned to me by heaven' (*F*, p. 191). Shortly after making this pronouncement, Frankenstein becomes mortally ill, and although he does not relent from his own purpose, he says to Walton, 'Seek happiness in tranquillity, and avoid ambition [...] Yet why do I say this? I have myself been blasted in these hopes, yet another might succeed' (*F*, p. 193). Frankenstein's vacillation here could be seen as reflecting Shelley's own uncertainty. She, like Frankenstein, is intensely drawn to an ideology, but is wary of the potential dangers.

Shelley's scepticism about certain elements of radical politics is something which she revisits throughout her career, particularly in the midst of what Cronin calls the 'lacuna' of literary history. In her novel, *The Last Man* (1826), Shelley presents a vision of 21st-century England in which the characters of Adrian and Lord Raymond—thinly-veiled portraits of Percy Shelley and Lord Byron—are members of a ruling elite in a republican state. They strive to rescue humanity from a devastating plague, but ultimately fail, leaving only one survivor. The novel can be read as a strong critique of the Godwinian model of politics, or even of Percy Shelley's projected utopias in poems such as *Queen Mab* (1813). Kari Lokke argues that 'its refusal to place humanity at the centre of the universe, its questioning of our privileged position in relation to nature [...] constitutes a profound and prophetic challenge to Western humanism', adding that the novel 'attacks Enlightenment faith in the inevitability of progress through collective efforts'.[9] In essence, *The Last Man* projects the failure of radical Romantic politics in the 1820s into a distant future setting. In a journal entry of 1824, Shelley more or less confirms this reading of the novel by comparing her own experience, following the death of Percy Shelley in 1822, with that of the last living man on Earth: 'The last man! Yes, I may well describe that solitary being's feelings, feeling myself the last relic of a beloved race, my companions extinct before me'.[10]

*Frankenstein*, however, begun ten years before *The Last Man* was published, is never so direct in its criticism. If one reads Mary Shelley's letters during her time in Geneva in 1816, it is clear that she was indeed passionately committed to many of her father's and lover's political principles. In a letter she wrote to her half-sister, Fanny Imlay, she scoffed at the narrow elitism of England, while admiring the more egalitarian conditions of Switzerland:

> There is more equality of classes here than in England. This occasions a greater freedom and refinement of manners among the lower orders than we meet with in our own country. I fancy the haughty English ladies are greatly disgusted with this consequence of republican institutions.[11]

And yet, *Frankenstein* remains implicitly critical of certain aspects of William Godwin's and Percy Shelley's philosophies, and the manner in which they pursued them. In this sense, the novel is caught between two contrary impulses.

The notion that *Frankenstein* presents a narrative of confused, potentially contradictory ideas is not a new one. Chris Baldick, for example, suggests that the text has an 'abundant excess of meanings which the novel cannot stably accommodate'.[12] Baldick's analysis, however, implies that this is an accident of execution on Shelley's part—that she is trying to say too many things in a restricted space, or that she simply does not know what she is doing. If we turn to the novel's preface, however, Shelley provides a pre-emptive rebuttal to this accusation:

> The opinions which naturally spring from the character and situation of the hero are by no means to be conceived as existing always in my own conviction; nor is any inference justly to be drawn from the following pages as prejudicing any philosophical doctrine of any kind.
>
> (*F*, p. 2)

To put it another way, if *Frankenstein* appears to have no dominant message, or 'philosophical doctrine', it is not because Shelley fails to articulate one, but rather because she has no intention of providing one. She avoids associating herself with the 'hero'—whom she takes care not to explicitly identify as Victor Frankenstein—because she is not concerned with promoting her own convictions over others. From the outset, Shelley frames *Frankenstein* as an ambivalent space, a text which deliberately resists conclusive judgements.

Nowhere is this sense of ambivalence more prominent than in the character of Frankenstein's creation. Of all the characters in the novel, the Creature is the most fundamentally divided, and indeed the most Miltonic. When he confronts Frankenstein in the mountains, and recounts his experiences following his departure from Ingolstadt, he recalls reading a copy of *Paradise Lost*, and how he related to the characters in the poem:

> Like Adam, I was apparently united by no link to any other being in existence; but his state was far different from mine in every other respect. He had come forth from the hands of God a perfect creature, happy and prosperous, guarded by the especial care of his creator; he was allowed to converse with, and acquire knowledge from, beings of a superior nature: but I was wretched, helpless, and alone. Many times I considered Satan as the fitter emblem of my condition; for often, like him, when I viewed the bliss of my protectors, the bitter gall of envy rose within me.
>
> (*F*, p. 108)

Throughout the novel, the Creature continually oscillates between these divided self-images. As he recalls the early days of his life, wandering through the forest outside Ingolstadt, he switches between parallels of Satan and Adam in the beginning of *Paradise Lost*. He suggests that while one forest hut seemed as 'divine a retreat as Pandemonium appeared to the daemons of hell', another resembled a 'paradise' (*F*, pp. 108–109). As Gilbert and Gubar have it, '*Frankenstein* is ultimately a mock Paradise Lost' in which the Creature, and at times others, 'play all the neo-biblical parts over and over again'.[13] This vacillation between identities gives the Creature a sense of uncertain potential—a feeling that he has an equal capacity for good or evil which is dependent on how the world treats him. As he himself puts it: 'I was once benevolent and good; misery made me a fiend. Make me happy, and I shall again be virtuous' (*F*, p. 124).

*Frankenstein* once again engages with William Godwin's philosophy here through the notion of the perfectibility of mankind and the pursuit of intellectual and moral self-development. In his great political and philosophical tract, *Enquiry Concerning Political Justice and its Influence on Morals and Happiness* (1793), Godwin posits that 'the characters of men originate in their external circumstances'.[14] On this basis, he argues that if people were free from the oppressive power structures which seek to regulate people and society, such as governments and monarchies, and were properly educated, they would naturally move to an ethical and intellectual position that was mutually beneficial for all citizens:

> The supreme power in a state ought not, in the strictest sense, to require anything of its members, that an understanding sufficiently enlightened would not prescribe without such interference.[15]

The creature's insistence that he can be made happy and virtuous by the external actions of Victor Frankenstein would, at first, appear to support this Godwinian notion of moral and intellectual development.

However, if one examines the particular details of the Creature's early development, Shelley appears to disrupt, or at least question, the logic of her father's assertions. It is significant to note that the Creature's first exposures to history and literature are all works which are in some way aligned with politically radical, republican, or Romantic ideas. He eavesdrops on Felix—one of the cottagers whose shed he hides within during his early life—reading Volney's *Ruins of Empires*, a French polemic on the governments of ancient civilisations published in 1791, a text which was highly influential among both English and French radicals. The three books which the Creature possesses himself are *Paradise Lost*, Goethe's *Sorrows of Werter*, and Plutarch's *Parallel Lives*. All of these texts engage with the nature of individuals and their relation to morality and society. Goethe's *Sorrows of Werter* has a narrative focused on solitude and unrequited love, whereas Plutarch's *Parallel Lives* has a particular emphasis on the personal virtue of individuals. In effect, he is 'reared on radical idealism'.[16] And yet, despite these powerful cultural influences—the kind of external influences which Godwin believed shape a person's nature—the Creature ultimately develops into an 'evil' character.

Of course, one could argue that the Creature has a great deal of other influences, not least his barbaric treatment by the first humans he encounters, who chase him with violence, as does Felix the cottager when he eventually discovers him. And yet, the Creature's responses, which range from burning down the cottage to the eventual pursuit and murder of all of Victor Frankenstein's loved ones, are such a dramatic reaction that it calls into question how equal the Creature's capacities for good and evil truly are. Frankenstein himself avers that the Creature has a natural, or rather unnatural, propensity for wickedness. He states that the Creature's 'soul is as hellish as his form, full of treachery and fiend-like malice' (*F*, p. 184).

This fear that destructiveness could be as innate in human nature as the desire for social cohesion is especially significant when viewed in its historical context. Shelley began composing *Frankenstein* in 1816, just a year after Waterloo. Europe had emerged from a period of incredible violence and tyranny that could trace its beginnings to the radical idealism of the 1790s. Some critics, such as Ronald Paulson, have even suggested that *Frankenstein* is itself a literary reimagining of the French Revolution and Napoleonic Wars:

> Mary Shelley's *Frankenstein* [...] was to some extent a retrospect on the whole process through Waterloo, with the Enlightenment-created monster leaving behind its wake of terror and destruction across France and Europe, partly because it had been disowned and misunderstood and partly because it was created unnaturally by reason rather than love.[17]

Whether or not one wishes to go that far, it is certainly true that the violence of the French Revolution carries an implicit threat throughout *Frankenstein*, and perhaps offers the clearest understanding of the divisions contained within the novel. Shelley deliberately avoids revealing dates, but there are small hints that the novel is set during the revolutionary years of the 1790s. In one of the more revealing passages of the novel, the threat of a French invasion in Switzerland is obliquely referred to:

> we saw the mighty Jura opposing its dark side to the ambition that would quit its native country, and an almost insurmountable barrier to the invader who should wish to enslave it.
>
> (*F*, p. 169)

The violence of revolution and of the Napoleonic Wars represents the ultimate consequence of misguided and overreaching radicalism. The divided narrative voices of Walton and Frankenstein demonstrate the fine margins of where an obsessive desire to become the 'benefactors' of mankind can lead. Frankenstein has opportunities to turn away from his obsessive quest for human perfection, but by the time he does it is too late. It is implicit, though not guaranteed, that if Walton had continued his voyage to the North Pole both he and his crew would have died. The fundamentally divided Creature, torn between his contrary self-images of Adam and Satan, is likewise defined by his uncertain potential. Even at the end of the novel, where the Creature vows to commit suicide, the event itself is unconfirmed, leaving open the possibility that he could continue his campaign of terror.

*Frankenstein*, then, is a novel riddled with uncertainty and Miltonic divisions. And yet, despite this, it is a novel that is unafraid to confront its own apparent lack of a conclusive message. Written in 1816, *Frankenstein* lies less than a decade from the border of Cronin's lacuna of literary history. Shelley could not, of course, have known that with the deaths of Byron, Keats, and Percy Shelley only a few years away, 'the spirit of the age' as she knew it—and Hazlitt immortalised it—was drawing swiftly towards its close. And yet it was obvious that the world was changing. Napoleon had been defeated, Europe was finally in a relative state of peace, and on a personal level Mary Shelley was emerging as a fully formed writer. The future of the political and cultural landscape of the country was unknowable. In *Frankenstein*, Shelley offers us a vision of disaster, but it is located in the past. The future, like Frankenstein's Creature, has an unknown capacity for good or ill.

## Notes

1 Mary Shelley, *Frankenstein*, ed. by Marilyn Butler (London: Pickering Women's Classics, 1993), Title page. All subsequent page references are from this edition, abbreviated as '*F*', and are given in parentheses after quotations in the text.
2 Sandra M. Gilbert and Susan Gubar, *The Madwoman in the Attic: The Woman Writer and the Nineteenth-century Literacy Imagination* (New Haven: Yale University Press, 1984).
3 It is important to note that I am focusing on the first version of *Frankenstein*, originally published in 1818, rather than the revised version published in 1831. This is because I am explicitly interested in Shelley's ideas pre-Cronin's lacuna. Readers interested in the differences between the two versions may wish to consult the following: James O'Rourke, 'The 1831 Introduction and Revisions to "Frankenstein": Mary Shelley Dictates Her Legacy', *Studies in Romanticism*, 38: 3 (1999), 365–85.
4 Beth Lau, 'Romantic Ambivalence in *Frankenstein* and *The Ancient Mariner*', in *Fellow Romantics: Male and Female British Writers, 1790–1835*, ed. by Beth Lau (Milton: Routledge, 2009), pp. 71–97 (p. 83).
5 William Godwin, *Enquiry Concerning Political Justice and its Influence on Morals and Happiness* (London: G. G. J. and J. Robinson, 1793), p. 100, https://ebooks.adelaide.edu.au/g/godwin/william/enquiry/index.html [accessed July 2024]
6 Catherine C. Hill-Miller, *My Hideous Progeny: Mary Shelley, William Godwin and the Father-Daughter Relationship* (Newark: University of Delaware Press, 1995), p. 59.
7 Jane Blumberg, *Mary Shelley's Early Novels* (London: MacMillan, 1993), p. 30.
8 Irene Taylor and Gina Luria, 'Gender and Genre: Women in British Romantic Literature', in *What Manner of Woman: Essays in English and American Life and Literature*, ed. by Marlene Springer (New York: New York University Press), pp. 98–128 (p. 121).
9 Kari Lokke, '*The Last Man*', in *The Cambridge Companion to Mary Shelley*, ed. by Esther Schor (Cambridge: Cambridge University Press, 2003), pp. 116–29.
10 Mary Shelley, 'Journal Entry May 1824', in *Mary Shelley: Journal*, ed. by Frederick L. Jones (Norman: University of Oklahoma Press, 1947), p. 193.
11 Mary Shelley, 'Letter to Fanny Imlay, 1 June 1816', in *The Letters of Mary Wollstonecraft Shelley*, ed. by Betty T. Bennett (London: The John Hopkins Press, 1980), p. 21.
12 Chris Baldick, *In Frankenstein's Shadow: Myth, Monstrosity, and Nineteenth-century Writing* (Oxford: Oxford University Press, 1987), p. 33.
13 Sandra M. Gilbert and Susan Gubar, *The Madwoman in the Attic: The Woman Writer and the Nineteenth-century Literacy Imagination* (New Haven: Yale University Press, 1984), pp. 229–30.

14 William Godwin, *Enquiry Concerning Political Justice and its Influence on Morals and Happiness* (London: G. G. J. and J. Robinson, 1793), p. 38, https://ebooks.adelaide.edu.au/g/godwin/william/enquiry/index.html [accessed July 2024]
15 William Godwin, *Enquiry Concerning Political Justice and its Influence on Morals and Happiness* (London: G. G. J. and J. Robinson, 1793), p. 109, https://ebooks.adelaide.edu.au/g/godwin/william/enquiry/index.html [accessed July 2024]
16 Jane Blumberg, *Mary Shelley's Early Novels* (London: MacMillan, 1993), p. 21.
17 Ronald Paulson, 'Gothic Fiction and the French Revolution', *ELH*, 48: 3 (1981), 532–54 (545).

# 4 'Neither Whig, Tory, Radical, nor Destructionist'

## *The Private Memoirs and Confessions of a Justified Sinner* and the 'Polydoxy' of James Hogg

*The Private Memoirs and Confessions of a Justified Sinner* (1824) is a novel which is, like *Frankenstein*, positioned on the cusp of Cronin's 'lacuna' of literary history. Indeed, Hogg's novel resembles *Frankenstein* in a number of interesting ways. The two novels share the same Miltonic divisions in their narrative and characters, as well as a thematic focus on ambition, temptation, and fallenness. Both novels are also deeply political. Drawing explicit parallels with *Frankenstein*, Richard Walker suggests in his book, *Labyrinths of Deceit* (2007), that *Confessions* 'articulates a nineteenth-century crisis of identity', which extends into politics, society, and literature.[1] In *Frankenstein*, we see this crisis via the preoccupation with the radical ideology of Mary Shelley's immediate circle of friends, family, and fellow writers. *Confessions* also responds to its political environment, but in a way that differs sharply from *Frankenstein*. Whereas Shelley's novel expresses an anxiety about the failure of a single coherent political philosophy to encompass all of her beliefs, Hogg's novel revels in the idea of plurality and ambiguity as a defence against the dangers of fundamentalism. This manifests itself, in part, through a deliberate resistance to conclusion, forcing readers to interrogate their own ideologies as well as those offered up by the novel's characters and plot.

In this respect, the novel further recalls *Paradise Lost*. I have already discussed the manner in which the competing narrative voices of that poem invite the reader to interact with the text in sometimes contrary ways. This point is more deeply developed in Stanley Fish's well-known book, *Surprised by Sin* (1967), where he posits that Milton designs his poem such that the reader is rendered 'a participant in the action', experiencing the temptations and falls of the different characters in a manner that forces them to reflect on their personal moral position.[2] In this chapter, I shall argue that Hogg's novel does something similar. While it is in some respects a rather specific response to the increasingly fractious and polarised political and literary landscape of 1820s Britain, with a particular onus on Hogg's own Scottish, Tory circle, *Confessions* also has a far broader resonance. By leading his reader through the ruinous consequences of one man's commitment to a stubborn, ideological narrowness of outlook, the book acts as a cautionary tale to those who do

DOI: 10.4324/9781003527466-7

not open themselves up to the kind of acceptance of doubt and plurality that *Confessions* requires of its readers.

Politically, James Hogg is usually positioned by critics and historians—and indeed positions himself at times—as a Tory, or at the very least Tory-leaning. And yet, giving a truly precise label to Hogg's own personal and political loyalties is a notoriously awkward thing to do. Karl Miller gives an impression of the difficulty of the task, remarking that Hogg was a man of many apparently conflicting sympathies:

> Hogg was a poet and a peasant, a poor man who was also a personality, a star. A devotee both of war and peace, of animals and of their destruction, of truth and of lies, openness and disguise, of reason and imagination, simplicity and sophistication, chastity and license. Both a Tory and a Whig, a Cavalier and a Covenanter, a Jacobite and a Hanoverian.[3]

Hogg himself, in a diatribe entitled 'A Screed on Politics' (1835), appears to enunciate his political identity as one that is more nuanced than party politics can allow: 'I am neither Whig, Tory, Radical, nor Destructionist, but merely a sincere lover of his country'.[4]

The majority of Hogg's contradictions seem to stem from his background. As a youth in Ettrick, he was forced by his father's bankruptcy into working as a farm labourer, herding sheep and cattle. Unlike many of his Romantic contemporaries he received limited conventional schooling, having attended formal education in short spells amounting to perhaps six months in total.[5] Despite this relatively humble upbringing, Hogg did seem to tend in favour of the conservative Tories, rather than the more liberal Whigs. Indeed, as a regular contributor to one of the flagship publications of Tory principles, *Blackwood's Magazine*, Hogg often became a figure of ridicule among his more privileged fellows. Known as the 'Ettrick Shepherd' by his peers at the magazine, a soubriquet he cultivated for himself, the relationships he formed were often affectionate but also tinged with an element of condescension. Ian Duncan identifies one particular article by John Wilson, ostensibly a review of one of Hogg's novels, *The Three Perils of Woman* (1823), but in reality an 'attack on Hogg's literary character'. Duncan describes this moment as the 'culminating offence in a pattern of mockery and rejection by Hogg's peers at *Blackwood's*'.[6]

Class divisions of the kind Hogg experienced were, in my view, inextricably tied to the fraught political atmosphere of the time in which he lived. The 'immense public drama' of Hogg's literary lifetime was the attempt to secure an improved Parliament, with the eventual consequence of the passing of the Reform Bill in 1832, bringing 43,000 working- or middle-class people into the electorate.[7] Hogg's own position in this is interesting. As he was an avowed Tory, one might assume his natural stance towards this kind of constitutional reform would have been one of conservatism and caution, but his own background and character made him an egalitarian, on an emotional level at least. William Chambers, the publisher and bookseller, remarked that 'It did not seem as if he had the slightest veneration for any one more than another whom he addressed, no matter what was their rank or position'.[8]

Given this resistance to cohesion between his character and his politics, it is difficult to argue that any of Hogg's works are categorically in favour of, or opposed to, any particular group or ideology. Indeed, it is especially difficult regarding *Confessions*, a novel which is predicated upon multiplicity and uncertainty, and is filled by a cacophony of divergent and opposing voices, genres contained within genres, and a range of narrators and sub-narrators united only by their unreliability. Even described in its simplest terms, the novel is defined by contradiction and deception. George and Robert are two brothers, uncertain of whether they share the same father—one is raised as a not-very-devout Catholic Tory, the other a fanatical Calvinist Whig. Robert meets a stranger who can adopt exact likenesses of anyone, but most often the guise of Robert himself, and together they murder George, though the exact version of how this transpires is likewise uncertain and the subject of differing accounts. Finally, Robert is driven insane by his new friend, Gil-Martin, and commits suicide at his behest. All of these events are framed by the 'Editor's Narrative', in fact written by Hogg himself, which explains the fictional provenance of the Memoirs and casts further uncertainty as to the 'true' nature of the events described.

John Plotz recognises this apparent lack of clarity in Hogg's work as a deliberate act on the author's part—a demonstration that one piece of fiction can stably contain the clash of apparently contradictory philosophies:

> Hogg produced texts with central mysteries that lend themselves to various sorts of explanation — Satanic possession, individual madness, collective delusion, or simply distorting the lens of history — but which finally resist the triumph of any one explanatory schema over its alternatives. Hogg practiced what could be called (on the model of Bakhtin's polyglossia) polydoxy, which stages the intersection of profoundly disjunctive belief systems within a single piece of fiction.[9]

*Confessions* expresses Hogg's own personal 'polydoxy'—he is himself an intersection of contradictions. Crucially, the novel demonstrates how this is, in fact, a healthier and more sustainable mode of being than to be wedded to a single, entirely unshakable philosophy. Just as *Paradise Lost* can sustain a heroic, persuasive Satan within a clearly Christian poem, so too can Hogg and his works sustain and encourage the kind of contradictions that invite the reader to interrogate their own perspective in the way that Fish describes.

The most obvious way in which Hogg does this is through his engagement with Calvinism. Hogg's criticism of the Calvinist notion of predestination provides an allegorical vehicle for more wide-ranging concerns. His treatment of the Calvinist principle of an Elect group, predestined for Paradise, reflects his dissatisfaction with the exclusionary narrowness and elitism of both the political and literary establishment. For instance, Cates Baldridge suggests that Hogg's implicit criticism of Calvinism serves as a 'metaphorical critique' of the 'hyper-partisanship' of the Edinburgh magazine set, of which he himself was a part.[10] In my opinion, this analysis can be extended to a more general condemnation of political and philosophical fundamentalism.

A good example of this is found in the relationship between Robert Wringhim and George Colwan. In these two characters we see a potential for a mutually constructive meeting of two world views—two brothers, raised with totally different beliefs, but united by common heritage. Unfortunately, this possibility is never allowed to be explored, as Robert has been indoctrinated into a philosophy of elitism and division. According to the Calvinist principle of predestination, Robert is told that he is one of 'the just made perfect [...] adopted among the number of God's children', and therefore superior to his brother.[11] His elitist, narrow outlook stands in stark contrast with Hogg's own sense of personal and political identity—the idea that growth and understanding is achieved by moving beyond the predetermined boundaries of one's upbringing.

If we turn to his poetry, we can see how this has direct parallels with Hogg's view of the country's literary elite. Louis Simpson wrote that Hogg's poetry suffered from a confusion over whether he was writing for 'Tory Edinburgh or his own "common people"', but I am inclined to think that this view misunderstands Hogg's deliberate resistance to such binaries.[12] In his collection of poems, *The Poetic Mirror* (1816), Hogg parodied a number of other Romantic poets of varying backgrounds. In 'The Stranger', Hogg assumes the voice of William Wordsworth, once considered a radical free-thinker, but by 1816 very much a conservative, elitist voice. In this Wordsworthian guise, Hogg discusses the failings of an unidentified 'Border Minstrel' with some other poets, including one referred to as 'The Shepherd':

> You must acknowledge this your favourite
> Hath more outraged the purity of speech,
> The innate beauties of our English tongue,
> For amplitude and nervous structure famed,
> Than all the land beside, and therefore he
> Deserves the high neglect which he has met
> From all the studious and the thinking—those
> Unsway'd by low caprices of age,
> The scorn of reason, and the world's revile.[13]

The Wordsworth character's reluctance to accommodate difference and variety here is telling. The Border Minstrel is a thinly veiled guise for Walter Scott, a writer widely known for his use of Scots dialect and the influence of a 'common' oral tradition, something Hogg himself makes use of in *Confessions*. The Wordsworth character's 'comically pretentious' attack on this 'impurity' corresponds with Robert Wringhim's own obsession with perfection and status.[14] Both of these cases reinforce Hogg's message that elitist groups which exclude difference and variety only conspire to deprive themselves of a richness and diversity of experience, making them appear aloof and somewhat ridiculous.

If we compare this parody of Wordsworth with the image Hogg seeks to cultivate for himself in *Confessions*, we see the extent to which he feels, or perhaps wishes to appear, an outsider from this elite group. In what amounts to a self-portrait—appearing as a character within his own faux Editor's Narrative—Hogg gives himself a broad Scots dialect and a haughty disdain for anything unrelated to the trade of livestock. On being questioned about the events chronicled in *Confessions*, he remarks that any interest in the exploits of a long dead suicide 'was a queer fancy for a woo-stapler to tak' (*C*, p. 204). The conflict with that statement, of course, is that Hogg is in fact both Editor and author of the novel, creating a multi-layered narrative frame which 'provides an auto-critique or gloss' upon the central text, thus effectively entering into dialogue' with his own novel in a way that recalls the divided, interacting narratives of *Paradise Lost* and the other texts under discussion in this book.[15]

As I shall elucidate later, the whole of *Confessions* is freckled with cameo appearances of people Hogg knew and other similarly personal, autobiographical touches that build up this sense of narrative wall breaking. And yet, when these moments are added together, they give anything but a coherent sense of Hogg's character and beliefs, leaving one with a conflicting image of the man and his world views, and the sense that Hogg's identity has 'become increasingly dispersed and unstable'.[16] Both he and his novel certainly lack the 'purity' and coherence which his faux-Wordsworth demands.

If *Confessions*, then, is a novel which denigrates the pursuit of purity and perfection, it is also a novel which elevates pragmatism and moderation to high virtues. One proponent of this in the novel is the preacher, Rev. Blanchard. Speaking with Robert about religion, he asserts that 'there is nothing so dangerous to man as the wresting of its principles, or forcing them beyond their due bounds: this is of all others the readiest way to destruction' (*C*, p. 109). Blanchard's message is one of moderation, caution, and a certain amount of humility. Shortly after this intervention, Blanchard is murdered by Robert and Gil-Martin when the latter convinces his companion that Blanchard is a 'Wretched contravertist' (*C*, p. 112). The incident is illustrative of the irrationality of a debate where one side is determinedly wedded to their perspective.

It is equally significant to note that underlying Blanchard's moderate attitude is a natural and unasked for kindness. Blanchard did not have to offer Robert advice but felt compelled to do so, nonetheless. *Confessions* is a novel mostly remembered for the instances of extreme wickedness it contains, but it also accommodates its fair share of generosity. In particular, these acts tend to come from the lower-class, 'rustic' characters in the novel, such as the 'poor hind' who allows Robert to sleep on a bed of rushes in his cottage. This man's virtue is highlighted by his unique ability to repel the demons which plague the protagonist: 'a power protected that house superior to those that contended for, or had the mastery over me' (*C*, p. 194). Interestingly, this is yet another autobiographic interjection by Hogg who, by some accounts, slept on a bed of rushes in his shepherding bothy in the Scottish borders.[17] This romanticising of the poor gives us a further insight into why Hogg chose to cultivate his Ettrick Shepherd persona, as he seeks to claim a positive cultural heritage to counter the perception of him as too vulgar and common to be poet.

Indeed, Douglas Mack makes the point that much of the tension between Hogg's political loyalties and his background stem from a perception of him as belonging to a superstitious, un-sophisticated culture:

> [The] intellectual elite of Hogg's era had a tendency to make a simple binary distinction between the world of the Enlightenment (seen as straightforwardly true and valid), and pre-Enlightenment culture (seen as backward and deluded). In this context, there was a tendency for Hogg himself to be viewed as someone not to be taken entirely seriously: an interesting and exotic specimen, no doubt, but decidedly a backwoodsman, the product of a primitive stage of social evolution.[18]

The strange power of the old man and his cottage clearly speaks to a superstitious, pre-enlightenment sensibility, but in a typically contradictory way it is Hogg himself, in his guise as the Editor, who brings incidents such as these under scrutiny. The closing passages of the Editor's Epilogue question every aspect of the events described, asserting that it is 'impossible that these scenes could ever have occurred', attributing most of the events related in 'The Memoir' as either lies, fiction, 'dreaming or madness' (*C*, p. 209). And indeed, the Shepherd Hogg who appears as a character in the Editor's Narrative possesses little in the way of rustic mystique, concerned only for his 'paulies' (*C*, p. 204), and largely uninterested in the apparently magical preservation of the corpse he claims to have found.

In this sense, the narrative division of *Confessions* is as vital to unlocking the novel's meaning as it is in *Paradise Lost* or *Frankenstein.* As with both of those texts, there is a juxtaposition of voices which invites readers to question their feelings and assumptions on every point. The sceptical, rational voice of the Editor's Narrative surrounds the far more outlandish Sinner's Narrative, with its seductive, exciting, improbable content. What *Confessions* achieves in this is a disruption of the binary assumptions that Mack identifies, compelling the reader to reflectively interact with the text, as in Fish's reading of *Paradise Lost.* It would have been simple for Hogg to create his novel on purely oppositional lines, with the well-educated, well-off, though spiritually twisted Robert counterbalanced by the ignorant but noble mysticism of the poor, presenting an easily digestible moral narrative to his readers. To do this, however, would merely serve to reinterpret the perception of pre- and post-enlightenment binaries: it would not dismiss them altogether.

What *Confessions* offers us instead is a kind of 'polydoxy'—one that rejects the idea that groups in society share single bloc identities into which they can be pigeonholed. In terms of the novel's narrators, Robert is the voice of education and orthodoxy, as well as the voice of superstition and wonder. The Editor is at once the sceptical voice of the establishment, and yet we know that he is merely a guise for the lowly Ettrick Shepherd. Neither party quite fits into the box to which one might feel they belong, rejecting the idea that narratives and characters ought to cohere and conform to single identities.

In Robert's case, unfortunately, it is his unwillingness and/or inability to recognise the value of his contradictions which ultimately damns him. His relationship with Gil-Martin is the central symbol of this destructive narrow-mindedness. When they first meet, Gil-Martin assumes the physical appearance of Robert, but also avers that he has the same spirit and beliefs:

> 'You think I am your brother', said he; 'or that I am your second self. I am indeed your brother, not according to the flesh, but in my belief of the same truths, and my assurance in the same mode of redemption, than which, I hold nothing so great and glorious on earth'.
>
> (*C*, p. 97)

Gil-Martin acts as a mirror to Robert's beliefs, but as the novel progresses we begin to see how with each reflection he intensifies and restricts the scope of Robert's understanding. Before he meets Gil-Martin, although he is still an unpleasant and conceited character, Robert is capable of appreciating worth beyond himself and his beliefs. In his schooldays he envies his curiously named classmate M'Gill's skill at drawing, and though he decries it as 'profane' (*C*, p. 91) still seeks to imitate it himself. Similarly, he is prepared to acknowledge those outside of his Elect group as being of a 'moral cast' (*C*, p. 108), such as Blanchard, and the Wringhims' servant, John Barnet. But the more he continues to associate only with Gil-Martin the more extreme and prejudicial he becomes, ultimately resulting in his series of murders.

In this way, Hogg describes the potentially dangerous consequences of ignoring or demeaning that which lies beyond one's own sphere—a model which might very easily be applied to politics as well as religion. Williston R. Benedict describes Gil-Martin and his influence on Robert as 'a projection into visible form' of his 'unresolvable inner conflicts'.[19] The tragedy that I believe Hogg wishes us to appreciate, however, is that such internal conflicts need *not* be unresolvable. The moment when Robert begins to appreciate his error, in a small way, is when he is told the story of Auchtermuchty by his servant. The story is told in Scots dialect and is very much grounded in a superstitious folk tradition. As the Editor might observe, the events it describes could not possibly be true, but its content is totally applicable to Robert's predicament, as it describes how a disguised Satan seduces a town full of people into evil. Robert denies that he is affected by this 'fool's idle tale', and yet concedes that it gives him a 'view of his own state, at which I shuddered' (*C*, p. 168). In other words, this exterior perspective gives him a new, albeit uncomfortable insight that he might not otherwise have gained. That Hogg chooses to formulate this exchange as one between an uneducated, working-class character and an educated, middle-class character emphasises the social and political relevance of this idea.

Mack provides a useful parallel for understanding Hogg's attempts in *Confessions* to mix political influences and social backgrounds together by comparing Hogg to another author, Charles Dickens:

> Hogg was a Tory who believed that it is foolish to throw 'the experience of ages aside as useless and unprofitable lumber'. Nevertheless, he shared Dickens's 'revolutionary' tendencies. Like Dickens, Hogg sympathised instinctively with 'the suffering and the humble side'; and, like Dickens, he believed that 'if men would behave decently the world would be decent'.[20]

The lines from Dickens perfectly capture the essence of *Confessions*. It is Robert Wringhim's decision to ignore the wisdom and experience of characters like Blanchard, or the local people and their 'old wives tales', which cause his demise. Those characters who practice decency—identified by Dickens as the prime virtue—such as the 'old hind' who shelters Robert, demonstrate the value of non-partisan generosity. Just as with Mary Shelley's *Frankenstein*, Hogg's novel does not seek to inflict an ideological perspective on its readers, but rather encourages them to question their own perceptions and prejudices. In this sense, both *Confessions* and *Frankenstein* continue the disruptive, deliberately oppositional narrative model of *Paradise Lost*. In both cases, these novels also appear to reflect that wider notion of a destabilisation of unified group identities—both cultural and political—which frames Richard Cronin's concept of the lacuna period of literary history.

In the next chapter, I will look ahead to Emily Brontë's *Wuthering Heights* (1847), a text which lies beyond the coronation of Queen Victoria and therefore beyond the defined further limit of Cronin's lacuna. And yet, it is a novel preoccupied with exactly those same concerns about divided and unstable cultural identities that we find in *Frankenstein* and *Confessions*, once again demonstrating the need for a more elastic understanding of this transitional literary period. *Wuthering Heights* is, however, different from *Confessions* and *Frankenstein* in one important respect. Whereas those two novels simply seek to expose and question the divisions which define the lacuna, *Wuthering Heights* attempts to understand and reconcile them.

## Notes

1 Richard J. Walker, *Labyrinths of Deceit: Culture, Modernity and Identity in the Nineteenth Century* (Liverpool: Liverpool University Press, 2007), p. 50.
2 Stanley Fish, *Surprised by Sin: The Reader in Paradise Lost* (London: Macmillan, 1967), p. 38.
3 Karl Miller, *Electric Shepherd: A Likeness of James Hogg* (London: Faber and Faber, 2003), p. 224.
4 James Hogg, 'A Screed on Politics', 1835, in *Contributions to Backwoods Magazine Volume 2: 1829–1835*, ed. by Thomas C. Richardson (Edinburgh: Edinburgh University Press, 2012), pp. 329–342 (p. 329).
5 Karl Miller, *Electric Shepherd: A Likeness of James Hogg* (London: Faber and Faber, 2003), p. 4.
6 Ian Duncan, *Scott's Shadow* (Princeton: Princeton University Press, 2007), p. 172.
7 Karl Miller, *Electric Shepherd: A Likeness of James Hogg* (London: Faber and Faber, 2003), p. 8.
8 William Chambers, *Memoir of William and Robert Chambers*, 13th Ed. (Edinburgh: W. & R. Chambers, 1884), p. 254.
9 John Plotz, 'Hogg and the Short Story', in the *Edinburgh Companion to James Hogg*, ed. by Ian Duncan and Douglas S. Mack (Edinburgh: Edinburgh University Press, 2012), pp. 113–21 (p. 115).
10 Cates Baldridge, 'Antinomian Reviewers: Hogg's Critique of Romantic-Era Magazine Culture in *The Confessions of a Justified Sinner*', *Studies in the Novel*, 43: 4 (2011), 385–405 (390).
11 James Hogg, *The Private Memoirs and Confessions of a Justified Sinner*, ed. by Karl Miller (London: Penguin Classics, 2006), pp. 95–96. All subsequent page references are from this edition, abbreviated as '*C*', and are given in parentheses after quotations in the text.
12 Louis Simpson, *James Hogg: A Critical Study* (Edinburgh: St Martin's Press, 1962), p. 57.
13 Hogg, 'The Stranger', in *The Poetic Mirror*, 2nd Ed. (London: Longman, 1817), p. 146, https://archive.org/details/cu31924104103779 [accessed July 2024]
14 Meiko O'Halloran, *James Hogg and British Romanticism: A Kaleidoscopic Art* (Basingstoke: Palgrave MacMillan, 2016), p. 1.
15 Richard J. Walker, *Labyrinths of Deceit: Culture, Modernity and Identity in the Nineteenth Century* (Liverpool: Liverpool University Press, 2007), p. 53.
16 Richard J. Walker, *Labyrinths of Deceit: Culture, Modernity and Identity in the Nineteenth Century* (Liverpool: Liverpool University Press, 2007), p. 55.
17 Karl Miller, *Electric Shepherd: A Likeness of James Hogg* (London: Faber and Faber, 2003), p. 1.
18 Douglas S. Mack, 'Hogg's Politics and the Presbyterian Tradition', in *The Edinburgh Companion to James Hogg*, ed. by Ian Duncan and Douglas S. Mack (Edinburgh: Edinburgh University Press, 2012), pp. 64–72 (p. 65).
19 Williston R. Benedict, 'A Story Replete with Horror', *The Princeton University Library Chronicle*, 44: 3 (1983), 246–51 (248).
20 Douglas S. Mack, 'Hogg's Politics and the Presbyterian Tradition', in *The Edinburgh Companion to James Hogg*, ed. by Ian Duncan and Douglas S. Mack (Edinburgh: Edinburgh University Press, 2012), p. 72.

# 5 *Wuthering Heights*

## 'As Different as a Moonbeam from Lightning'—Reconciling Romanticism and Victorianism

In discussing *Frankenstein* and *Confessions*, Part II has so far concentrated on texts which, according to Cronin's choice of dates, preface the lacuna of literary history—the period lying between the Romantic and Victorian periods of literature. This final chapter shall look to the other side of this historical gap, to Emily Brontë's *Wuthering Heights*. Published a decade after the coronation of Queen Victoria, *Wuthering Heights* is firmly situated in the Victorian period. This is a novel, however, which seeks to address its position in literary history and provide a bridge between Romantic and Victorian sensibilities—a feature which I believe ought to grant it a place within the bounds of Cronin's lacuna. Emily Rena-Dozier identifies this historical self-consciousness in her essay, 'Gothic Criticisms: *Wuthering Heights* and Nineteenth-Century Literary History' (2010), writing that:

> *Wuthering Heights* demonstrates perhaps more clearly than any other nineteenth-century novel the ways in which literary history participates in novelistic discourse, and its discomfort with the awareness that novels could also address literary history.[1]

The novel articulates this discomforting awareness by framing the transition from Romanticism to Victorianism as being a conflict of unregulated passion and superstition versus cold rationality and seriousness. In this sense, *Wuthering Heights* does not seek to promote Victorianism over Romanticism, or vice versa, but to pursue a further avenue—a reconciliation of two literary eras with apparently contrary ideological underpinnings, using the structures and tropes of Milton as her instrument.

Before explaining exactly how *Wuthering Heights* achieves this reconciliation of its Romantic and Victorian aspects, it is important to recognise that Emily Brontë and her peers were not, indeed could not, be fully cognisant of these two literary periods as distinct and defined eras. Donald Stone makes the pertinent observation that many of the great Victorian authors grew up 'during the period in which Romantic poetry and Scott's transformation of romance were being created', and so their own formations as writers were

DOI: 10.4324/9781003527466-8

inevitably informed by Romantic sensibilities.[2] With this in mind, it should not be entirely surprising that *Wuthering Heights* contains elements which might be considered Romantic. Indeed, in many respects it was the Victorians who first began the process of Romanticism's 'institutionalisation as a given of literary history'.[3] Brontë's novel should not, therefore, be understood as an attempt to resurrect Romanticism, but as an attempt to make sense of her own moment in literary history. It must be remembered that Brontë's novel sits only just beyond the uncertain period of Cronin's lacuna, and so the collision of Romantic and Victorian 'philosophies' that *Wuthering Heights* presents helps to reinforce the sense that this period of transition is finally ending, and that a new age has been embarked upon.

The principal way in which the conflict between Romantic passion and Victorian rationality is articulated in *Wuthering Heights* is through the positioning of Thrushcross Grange and Wuthering Heights—including their inhabitants—as opposing binaries. Gilbert and Gubar frame this oppositional division in firmly Miltonic terms:

> *Wuthering Heights* [...] is a radically corrective 'misreading' of Milton, a kind of Blakeian Bible of Hell, with the fall from heaven to hell transformed into a fall from a realm that conventional theology would associate with 'hell' (the Heights) to a place that parodies 'heaven' (the Grange).[4]

This sense of parodic symbolism is particularly true of Heathcliff and Edgar Linton who, in many ways, embody those qualities which we might regard as being representative of Romantic and Victorian ideologies. Heathcliff is in some respects an archetypal Romantic 'hero' taken from the mould of the Miltonic Satan. Indeed, from his first introduction to the Earnshaws, Heathcliff is swiftly associated with the diabolical, described as an 'imp of Satan' by Mrs Earnshaw.[5] The Romantic quality of this satanic connection is reflected in the contemporary critical response to *Wuthering Heights*. One reviewer even draws a direct parallel between Byron's Corsair and Heathcliff: 'Like the Corsair, and other such [...] heroes, he is "Linked to one virtue and a thousand crimes"'.[6] The one virtue referred to here is his consuming love for Cathy, a point to which I shall return later.

If Heathcliff is characterised as a devil, then one might imagine that his antipode, Edgar Linton, be cast as an angel, and in merely physical terms this is true. Heathcliff, the 'dirty, ragged, dark-haired' (*WH*, p. 29) child is initially envious of Edgar's appearance: 'I wish I had light hair and a fair skin, and was dressed and behaved well' (*WH*, p. 45). In an effort to achieve this, and to impress Cathy, Heathcliff asks Nelly to 'make me decent', declaring, 'I'm going to be good' (*WH*, p. 44). After some washing, combing, and encouragement, Nelly Dean manages to persuade him that a 'good heart' will help him to a 'bonny face', and he consequently loses 'his frown' and begins to look 'quite pleasant' (*WH*, p. 45). However, immediately upon meeting each other,

Edgar Linton makes a throwaway remark about the length of Heathcliff's hair, causing Heathcliff to abandon his new desire for goodness and attack Edgar. In the aftermath, Heathcliff is flogged by Hindley and swears to be revenged upon him: 'I shall pay Hindley back. I don't care how long I wait, if I can only do it, at last. I hope he will not die before I do!' (*WH*, p. 48). He scorns Nelly's suggestion that 'it is for God to punish', suggesting that God would not get the same 'satisfaction' that he would (*WH*, p. 48). In this rejection of his original desire to be 'good', and his stated quest for vengeance, Heathcliff once again conjures images of Milton's Satan. Like Heathcliff, Satan is forced to realise that he cannot match the 'transcendent brightness' (*PL*, I. 86) of angels, and so comforts himself with thoughts of vengeance:

> All is not lost – the unconquerable will,
> And study of revenge, immortal hate,
> And courage never to submit or yield
>
> (*PL*, I. 106–108)

In this way, the link between Heathcliff and those Romantic 'heroes' with whom he shares his Miltonic genealogy is cemented. Like Victor Frankenstein's Creature, Heathcliff is driven by self-loathing, and like Byron's Cain he is naturally impelled to struggle against authority. This Romantic commonality is noted by Chris Baldick who, drawing on the work of Lowry Nelson, suggests that *Wuthering Heights* fits into a group of 'diabolical' works from across the 19th century with a 'distinctive Romantic or mythic cast'.[7]

If the Romantic quality of Heathcliff is therefore clear, then the significance of Edgar Linton is less so. I suggested earlier that Edgar provides a binary rival for Heathcliff; a figure whom 'he hates not just as a rival but as an embodiment of everything effete and conventional' that he stands against.[8] And yet, in the early parts of the novel it is Hindley who is the chief target of Heathcliff's malice, with Edgar dismissed merely as a frail and 'petted' creature (*WH*, p. 38). The rivalry between the two characters only fully emerges when Cathy becomes romantically involved with Edgar, culminating in their marriage. It is this which sparks Heathcliff's desire for revenge, the only animus that seems to come close to inspiring the same level of passion as that which is aroused by Cathy herself. It is Cathy's deliberation on whether or not to marry Edgar that directly frames the rivalry of the two men as one between rationality and passion. Cathy's reasons for marrying Edgar are practical and coldly logical: Edgar is 'handsome', 'rich', and 'he loves me' (*WH*, p. 61). In contrast, she concludes that by any reasonable assessment a marriage to the poor and undistinguished Heathcliff would 'degrade' her (*WH*, p.63). And yet, her most passionate and intense comments are reserved for Heathcliff: 'Whatever our souls are made of, his and mine are the same, and Linton's is as different as a moonbeam from lightning, or frost from fire'—a vivid description which reinforces the notion of Heathcliff and Edgar as elemental contraries (*WH*, p. 63).

Through a modern prism we might reflexively suggest that Cathy's decision to marry 'against' love and to opt for pragmatism over passion is somehow perverse. However, we must remember that such marital alliances were far more commonplace in Victorian Britain. Arnold Shapiro notes that, throughout *Wuthering Heights*, 'love is presented in almost completely negative terms, set forth in opposition to society and its values, in a sense defined by those values'.[9] We see this sentiment illustrated in the contemporary critical response to the novel, where Cathy's rejection of Heathcliff in favour of Linton is one of the few points deemed positive and sensible. One reviewer remarked that once she is freed from the brutal passions of Wuthering Heights, a 'more gracious spirit comes over her, and she is gentle and more peaceful'.[10] And on a purely superficial level this reviewer is correct. Nelly Dean concedes that once Heathcliff has left, and Cathy is installed at Thrushcross Grange, that Cathy behaves 'infinitely better than I dared to expect', with little sign of her usually 'ill-natured and bad-tempered' demeanour (*WH*, p. 72). But what the reviewer fails to acknowledge is that this apparent serenity is an illusion. Cathy is not suddenly divested of her wild and passionate nature, but merely temporarily pacified by an environment which offers her no challenge or resistance. As Nelly puts it, it is not a case of the 'thorn bending to the honeysuckles, but the honeysuckles embracing the thorn' (*WH*, p. 72). One cannot argue that Cathy's relationship with Heathcliff is a healthy one, but it is at least not as superficial as that which she shares with Linton.

That sense of superficiality is another key to understanding the conflict of ideologies which *Wuthering Heights* seeks to illustrate. The false domestic harmony of the Lintons subversively mimics the model of the conventional Victorian novel, where good manners and the 'virtues of home and duty' are often celebrated above all else.[11] Indeed, the novel plays upon this idea from the beginning. When the narrator, Mr Lockwood, first encounters the inhabitants of Wuthering Heights he is the very epitome of superficial expectations, making a series of assumptions based on his ideas of how a family should be constructed. At first, he confuses Heathcliff and the younger Catherine for husband and wife, and then compounds his error by mistaking Hareton for the husband. All of Lockwood's judgements are made on the basis of surface appearance. Lockwood initially rejects the idea of Hareton and Catherine as a couple because the former seems so obviously of an inferior social class: 'his dress and speech were both rude, entirely devoid of the superiority observable in Mr and Mrs Heathcliff' (*WH*, p. 9).

One could argue that this is merely Brontë's way of injecting some comedy into what is a very melancholy novel, but it seems to me that Lockwood's shallowness raises a deeper point about social prejudice. Heathcliff is never warm to any character in the novel, save the elder Cathy. However, when he does express any admiration, however slight, it is never based on rank, bearing, or appearance, but on character. In her introduction to the 1850 edition of *Wuthering Heights*, Charlotte Brontë identifies this as the one of Heathcliff's few redeeming qualities:

> Heathcliff betrays one solitary human feeling, and that is *not* his love for Catherine, which is a sentiment fierce and inhuman [...] No; the single link that connects Heathcliff with humanity is his rudely confessed regard for Hareton Earnshaw — the young man whom he has ruined; and then his half-implied esteem for Nelly Dean.[12]

In a twisted sense, therefore, Heathcliff is an egalitarian, or if this is a step too far, he is certainly not an elitist or an establishment figure. For Daniela Garofalo, this is a quality mirrored in part by Cathy, who although clearly drawn by Edgar's wealth and status, ultimately regards family as 'not a matter of blood or marriage but of choice', holding 'the gypsy, slave, or dog' in a higher level of esteem than those with a more conventional expectation of her approval.[13] It is yet another way in which Heathcliff, and the qualities he draws out in Cathy, diverges from Edgar, the gentleman son of a magistrate who is meticulous in his distinctions between the classes. When Heathcliff returns from his travels to Thrushcross Grange, Edgar is made uncomfortable at the idea of entertaining a former 'ploughboy' in the parlour, suggesting the 'kitchen as a more suitable place for him' (*WH*, p. 75). This social and political contrast stirs the sense of a clash between a politically radical Romantic ideology and the more settled, domestic narratives associated with the Victorians.

Given that Heathcliff and Edgar are set up in this way, to be at odds on every issue, it might seem problematic to argue that *Wuthering Heights* offers a reconciliation of the conflict between Romanticism and Victorianism. If these characters are the avatars of these two cultural and literary eras, then their implacable opposition to each other seems to preclude any resolution. Rena-Dozier poses this dilemma well when she writes that '*Wuthering Heights* embodies the instability of nineteenth-century literary history's division between gothic and domestic novels'—a clash of styles so often situated in the space within and around Cronin's lacuna, where the 'gothic' represents a Romantic preoccupation with wild emotion and a tendency towards the lurid.[14] In her essay, Rena-Dozier frames this tension by recalling W. L. Cross's assertion that 'Romanticism had drunk immoderately of new emotions, and needed sharp castigation from [the] good sense' of more peaceful and domestic narratives like those of Jane Austen.[15] In my reading of *Wuthering Heights*, the answer to this seemingly irreconcilable clash of the domestic and the wild lies with Cathy—Heathcliff and Edgar love her. Each man is a symbol of apparently incompatible philosophies, but on this one issue they are united. They express their love in very different ways, and the nature of their love is different, but it is love, nonetheless. This love provides a pathway to understanding how Romantic passion and Victorian restraint can be brought together.

The chief faults of Heathcliff and Edgar are emblematic of the worst tendencies in Romanticism and Victorianism. Heathcliff is emotionally raw and prone to violence, whereas Edgar is repressed and superficial. However, there are instances in *Wuthering Heights* where these qualities are mitigated, or even actively reversed by each man's love for Cathy. For instance, Edgar, having shown unshakable restraint throughout the novel never to rise to the goading of Heathcliff and his open desire for intimacy with his wife, is only stirred to a show of true passion by an insult from Cathy. She accuses Edgar of having a 'weak nature', and of 'feigning more valour' than he possesses when he attempts to remove Heathcliff from Thrushcross Grange by peaceable means (*WH*, p. 90). As a result, Edgar's composure is cracked and he punches Heathcliff in the throat: a 'blow that would have levelled a slighter man' (*WH*, p. 91). One could never infer that Brontë's novel condones violence, but there is nevertheless a sense of righteousness about Edgar's reaction here. Indeed, the fact that Heathcliff is not really hurt by the assault underlines the point, because it is not the physical aspect of the punch that is significant, but the emotional propellant which launches it. It proves that Linton is capable of passion.

Conversely, Heathcliff's worst qualities are undoubtedly his cruelty and his propensity for violence. As with Edgar, at various points in the novel we see these negative aspects of his character mitigated by his love for Cathy. This is perhaps most apparent in his reluctance to beat the younger Catherine because of her resemblance to her mother:

> His black eyes flashed; he seemed ready to tear Catherine in pieces [...] when of a sudden, his fingers relaxed, he shifted his grasp from her head to her arm, and gazed intently at her face. Then he drew his hand over his eyes, stood a moment to collect himself apparently, and turning anew to Catherine, said with assured calmness —
>
> 'You must learn to avoid putting me in a passion, or I really shall murder you sometime!'
>
> (*WH*, p. 245)

The resemblance of Catherine to her mother, the one outlet for Heathcliff's passion that was in any way positive, brings out a moment of clarity in Heathcliff. He even uses the word 'passion' in its pejorative sense—almost an admission that his excess of passion is a failing in his character. This is a significant acknowledgment, especially given his constant lambasting of Edgar Linton as a 'milk-blooded coward' for his unwillingness to show passion through violent, extravagant acts (*WH*, p. 91).

However, it is not only the similarity between daughter and mother which deflates Heathcliff's violent temper, but also Hareton's similarity to Heathcliff. Richard Dellamora describes the connection between Heathcliff and Hareton as one of 'elective sonship', and it is certainly true that Hareton experiences their relationship in this way, describing Heathcliff as his 'father' even directly after the aborted attack on Catherine (*WH*, p. 245).[16] For Heathcliff, however, the relationship is not so domestic or familial. For Heathcliff, Hareton is the 'personification of my youth, not a human being' (*WH*, p. 247). In Hareton, Heathcliff sees the same qualities that he struggled with as a young man, his 'wild endeavours to hold my right, my degradation, my pride, my happiness, and my anguish' (*WH*, p. 247). This recognition of himself is so painful to Heathcliff that he confesses to Nelly that the mere sight of Hareton drives him near to insanity. He never fully articulates why this is, other than by suggesting it is bound up with his longing to see Cathy once again, implying a wish to return to the state of happiness they experienced together as youths.

In this regard it is not Hareton alone who so exorcises Heathcliff, but Hareton and Catherine together. In their mutually content relationship, Heathcliff is forced to witness what his life with Cathy might have been like under different circumstances. This vision is most forcefully imposed on Heathcliff in the short vignette of Catherine teaching Hareton to read, a scene which inspires a kind of reverie in Nelly Dean:

> they were thick again, in their several occupations, of pupil and teacher. You know, they both appeared, in a measure, my children: I had long been proud of one, and now, I was sure, the other would be a source of equal satisfaction. His honest, warm, and intelligent nature shook off rapidly the clouds of ignorance and degradation in which it had been bred; and Catherine's sincere commendations acted as a spur to his industry. His brightening mind brightened his features, and added spirit and nobility to their aspect. [...] each had so much of novelty to feel and learn, that neither experienced nor evinced the sentiments of sober disenchanted maturity.
> 
> (*WH*, p. 246)

I began this discussion by suggesting that *Wuthering Heights* seeks to reconcile Romanticism and Victorianism. This scene is the culmination of that reconciliation, aptly described by William A. Madden as a 'healthy binding' of competing energies that leads 'to constructive action'.[17] The ideological struggle between Romantic and Victorian, most clearly played out in the conflict between Heathcliff and Edgar, is dissolved here, as the best values of each ideology are combined. We see both the ambitious, egalitarian impulse of Romanticism, as Hareton is elevated from his position of servitude and ignorance, as well as the domestic harmony and gentility so central to the Victorian ideal. There is no feeling of conflict or tension here, no sense that Hareton will feel condescended to and erupt in a violent temper, nor that

Catherine will be unsettled by the passion of a mere 'ploughboy' and seek to restrain his impulse for betterment.

What *Wuthering Heights* achieves, then, is the completion of a transition. On a basic level, this is the culmination of the joining together of two families: the Earnshaws—including Heathcliff—and the Lintons. This joining is begun by Cathy and Edgar and concluded by the bonding of Hareton and Catherine—a generational handover. As Madden puts it:

> *Wuthering Heights* has provided the powerful experience of living twice through the same potentially traumatic circumstances, once ending in tragedy, but the second time with the energy bound and channelled into human wholeness and health.[18]

As I have sought to demonstrate, however, this rather simple dynastic transition also represents the resolution of an epic period of uncertainty, bridging two great eras of literary history. At the end of the novel, we are left with an image of three tombstones: Edgar's, Cathy's, and Heathcliff's, with either man on the opposing flank of the woman they loved. One could interpret this as a reification of Edgar and Heathcliff's implacable opposition to one another, even in death. Lockwood, however, can only infer a sense of peace from their mutual resting place, and cannot comprehend 'how anyone could imagine unquiet slumbers for the sleepers in that quiet earth' (*WH*, p. 258). Brontë's novel requires us to think about Romanticism and Victorianism in the same way, as two literary ideologies which can, in the end, lie comfortably with one another.

At the beginning of Part II, I set out to demonstrate that the literature of Richard Cronin's proposed lacuna period of literary history, through its use of divided voices and narratives, reflects a broader concern about the destabilisation of established cultural and political identities. However, the three novels which I have focused on all lie outside, or just on the periphery of, the dates of 1824 and 1840—the dates which Cronin offers as the boundaries of his proposed 'lacuna'. Cronin himself acknowledges the difficulty in successfully defining such limits, pointing out that literary history, like political history, 'tends not to stop when it is told to'.[19] What I have sought to argue for is that a greater elasticity ought to be applied when thinking about this transitional period between the Romantic and Victorian eras.

By offering fixed dates, albeit rather tentatively, Cronin seemingly implies that there is a mutually exclusive distinction between what lies within and without those dates. But this is a fallacy. *Frankenstein* and *Confessions* are both 'Romantic' novels sitting outside the 1824 boundary which Cronin sets. And yet, as I have argued, both novels latch onto that sense of uncertainty about identity which the idea of the 'lacuna' is predicated upon. Similarly, *Wuthering Heights* is absolutely Victorian, and the Brontë name is synonymous with Victorian literature more broadly. But, as with the earlier novels, those same concerns which define Cronin's 'lacuna' still arise, seven years beyond its stated parameters.

What this demonstrates is that literary history is not a series of static monoliths, but a dynamic and complex bundle of overlapping influences and ideas. Cronin is absolutely right to recognise that the interval between the Romantic and Victorian eras is a significant and distinctive moment in the evolution of British cultural identity. But what makes this period so interesting is not that it constitutes a unique buffer which separates two established blocs of literary history, but that it is a bridge which overlaps and unites them.

## Notes

1 Emily Rena-Dozier, 'Gothic Criticisms: *Wuthering Heights* and Nineteenth-Century Literary History', *ELH*, 77: 3 (2010), 757–75 (773).
2 Donald Stone, *The Romantic Impulse in Victorian Fiction* (Massachusetts: Harvard University Press, 1980), p. 2.
3 Joel Faflak and Julia M. Wright, *Nervous Reactions: Victorian Recollections of Romanticism* (Albany: State University of New York Press, 2004), p. 3.
4 Sandra M. Gilbert and Susan Gubar, *The Madwoman in the Attic: The Woman Writer and the Nineteenth-Century Literacy Imagination* (New Haven: Yale University Press, 1984), p. 189.
5 Emily Brontë, *Wuthering Heights: 1847 Text*, ed. by Richard Dunn (London: Norton, 2003), p. 32. All subsequent page references are from this edition, abbreviated as '*WH*', and are given in parentheses after quotations in the text.
6 'Unsigned Review of *Wuthering Heights*', *Examiner*, January 1848, in *The Brontës: The Critical Heritage*, ed. by Miriam Allot (London: Routledge, 1974), p. 220.
7 Chris Baldick, *In Frankenstein's Shadow: Myth, Monstrosity, and Nineteenth-Century Writing* (Oxford: Oxford University Press, 1987), p. 43.
8 Vereen M. Bell, '*Wuthering Heights* and the Unforgivable Sin', *Nineteenth-Century Fiction*, 17: 2 (1962), 188–91 (190).
9 Arnold Shapiro, '*Wuthering Heights* as a Victorian Novel', *Studies in the Novel,* 1: 3 (1969), 284–96 (289).
10 'Unsigned Review of Wuthering Heights', *Britannia*, 15 January 1848, in *The Brontës: The Critical Heritage*, ed. by Miriam Allot (London: Routledge, 1974), p. 226.
11 Donald Stone, *The Romantic Impulse in Victorian Fiction* (Massachusetts: Harvard University Press, 1980), p. 113.
12 Charlotte Brontë, 'Introduction to 1850 Edition of *Wuthering Heights*', in *The Brontës: The Critical Heritage*, ed. by Miriam Allot (London: Routledge, 1974), p. 287.
13 Daniela Garofalo, 'Impossible Love and Commodity Culture in Emily Brontë's *Wuthering Heights*', *ELH*, 75: 4 (2008), 819–40 (p. 833).
14 Emily Rena-Dozier, 'Gothic Criticisms: *Wuthering Heights* and Nineteenth-Century Literary History', *ELH*, 77: 3 (2010), 757–75 (760).
15 W. L. Cross, *The Development of the English Novel* (London: MacMillan, 1899), p. 144.
16 Richard Dellamora, 'Earnshaw's Neighbour/ Catherine's Friend: Ethical Contingencies in *Wuthering Heights*', *EHL*, 74: 3 (2007), 535–55 (551).

17 William A. Madden, '*Wuthering Heights*: The Binding of Passion', *Nineteenth-Century Fiction*, 27: 2 (1972), 127–54 (147–48).
18 William A. Madden, '*Wuthering Heights*: The Binding of Passion', *Nineteenth-Century Fiction*, 27: 2 (1972), 127–54, (154).
19 Richard Cronin, *Romantic Victorians* (Basingstoke: Palgrave, 2002), p. 254.

# Conclusion

In writing this book, my principal aim has been to determine how *Paradise Lost*, and the 'Miltonic Ideas of the Fall' which I have identified, have been used as a template by Romantic and post-Romantic poets and authors seeking to write about revolution and transition. Revolution in this sense is not defined merely as a physical act of rebellion, but as the dramatic re-consideration of strongly held ideals: literary, political, and philosophical.

My argument rests upon three main strands. Firstly, that the first generation of Romantic poets used Miltonic Ideas of the Fall to explain, or even to justify, their change in political sensibilities. This can be seen in Blake's shift in focus from a 'corporeal' to a 'mental' war, or Coleridge and Wordsworth's adoption of an increasingly conservative political and philosophical identity in place of their former radicalism.

Secondly, that the so-called 'second-generation' Romantics, primarily illustrated through Byron and Keats, also adopted Milton and *Paradise Lost* as a means of rejecting their predecessors. Or, perhaps more accurately, seeking to usurp their predecessors' former position as the leading poetic voices of their time, using the idea of a necessary fall to justify this idea.

Thirdly and finally, I turn to the novelists who span Cronin's literary lacuna. I argue that these writers adopt a Miltonic model of competing dualities expressed through divided narratives and characters as way of interpreting the generational, political, socio-economic, and artistic shifts of this period.

All three of these strands are, of course, very closely intertwined in a number of different ways. However, it is my contention that the most important aspect that unites these three distinct arguments is that sense of competing forces, expressed in a style and form which is borrowed from Milton, but originates in feeling from the writers themselves. E. M. W Tillyard said of *Paradise Lost* that 'Milton speaks most of reason contending with passion and of the necessity of imposing limits on the desire of knowledge. Control has become more important than energy'.[1] He was writing about the contrast between the earlier books of *Paradise Lost,* which focus on Satan, and the latter ones which turn more towards the angels. However, the sentiment that defines this contrast—that of a battle between uncontrolled passion and

DOI: 10.4324/9781003527466-9

controlling reason—can be applied to each of the texts and writers I have discussed.

The first-generation Romantics' philosophical shift following the French Revolution can be seen as a move from radicalism to conservatism, but in their writing they prefer to frame this in terms of a move towards reason, and away from the flights of fancy of 'crudest youth' (*TP*, IX. 212). The second generation also believe themselves to be 'reasonable', but they define their role as poets as being, first and foremost, champions of passion. Indeed, Keats's philosophy of Negative Capability is predicated on the superior poetic force of mysterious and emotional beauty which 'obliterates all [other] consideration'. And finally, the Romantic novelists who span the so-called lacuna period can be seen as writers trying to find a means by which to understand, and bridge, the gap between the forces of reason and passion which would later come to define what we now call the Romantic and Victorian periods. This is expressed most clearly, perhaps, in *Wuthering Heights*, via the physical and emotional contest between Edgar Linton and Heathcliff.

In short, though this book has pursued an understanding of these texts through the prism of particular devices and techniques—Miltonic ideas of the Fall—there is a more primal, elemental connection between Romantic literature and Milton's *Paradise Lost*. Romantic writers may borrow from the model of the poem—its structure, its divisions, its narrative devices—but the thing which really binds them together is their central theme. But 'theme' is perhaps too dry a word: say rather that they share a soul. A soul that is defined not by a single strong message or conviction, but by a conflict of competing instincts. A battle between reason and passion for the soul of the writer.

## Note

1 E. M. W. Tillyard, *Milton* (London: Chatto & Windus, 1966), p. 247.

# Bibliography

## Primary Texts


Aeschylus, *Prometheus Bound, in Aeschylus: Plays: One*, trans. by Freideric Raphael and Kenneth McLeish (London: Methuen Drama, 1991).

Alighieri, Dante, *The Divine Comedy: Inferno, Volume I*, trans. by Charles S. Singleton (Princeton: Princeton University Press, 1970).

Blake, William, Appendix to *The Prophetic Books,* http://www.bartleby.com/235/343 .html [accessed July 2024]

Blake, William, *Songs of Innocence and of Experience*, ed. by Geoffrey Keynes (Oxford: Oxford University Press, 1967).

Blake, William, *William Blake: The Complete Poems,* ed. by Alicia Ostriker (New York: Penguin, 1977).

Brontë, Emily, *Wuthering Heights: 1847 Text*, ed. by Richard Dunn (London: Norton, 2003).

Byron, George Gordon, *Byron A Self-Portrait: Letters and Diaries, Vol II*, ed. by Peter Quennell (London: John Murray, 1950).

Byron, George Gordon, *Childe Harold's Pilgrimage*, ed. by Les Bowler and David Widger (Salt Lake City: Project Gutenberg), http://www.gutenberg.org/files/5131 /5131-h/5131-h.htm [accessed July 2024]

Byron, George Gordon, *Don Juan*, ed. by T. G. Steffan (Harmondsworth: Penguin, 1977).

Byron, George Gordon, *'Famous in my time': Byron's Letters and Journals, Volume 2, 1810–1812*, ed. by Leslie A. Marchand (London: John Murray, 1973).

Byron, George Gordon, *Lord Byron's Cain*, ed. by T. G. Steffan (Austin: University of Texas Press, 1968).

Byron, George Gordon, *The Vision of Judgement*, ed. by Mary Redman (Cambridge: Cambridge University Press, 1926).

Coleridge, Samuel Taylor, *Coleridge's Poetry and Prose*, ed. by Nicholas Halmi, Paul Magnuson, and Raimonda Modiano (London: Norton, 2004).

Coleridge, Samuel Taylor, *Table Talk: Volume II*, ed. by Carl Woodring (London: Routledge, 1990).

Godwin, William, *Enquiry Concerning Political Justice and its Influence on Morals and Happiness* (help_outline1793) https://ebooks.adelaide.edu.au/g/godwin/ william/enquiry/index.html [accessed July 2024]

Hogg, James, 'A Screed on Politics', in *Contributions to Backwoods Magazine Volume 2: 1829–1835*, ed. by Thomas C. Richardson (Edinburgh: Edinburgh University Press, 2012), pp. 329–342.

Hogg, James, *The Private Memoirs and Confessions of a Justified Sinner*, ed. by Karl Miller (London: Penguin Classics, 2006).

Hogg, James, 'The Stranger', in *The Poetic Mirror,* 2nd Ed. (London: Longman, 1817), pp. 131–154. https://archive.org/details/cu31924104103779 [accessed July 2024]

Keats, John, *Keats's Poetry and Prose*, ed. by Jeffrey Cox (London: Norton, 2009).

Keats, John, *The Letters of John Keats,* ed. by Maurice Forman (Oxford: Oxford University Press, 1952).

Milton, John, *Paradise Lost*, ed. by Gordon Teskey (London: Norton, 2005).

Milton, John, *The Areopagitica: A Speech for the Liberty of Unlicensed Printing* (London: MacMillan, 1904).

Milton, John, *The Readie and Easie Way* (London: 1660) http://eebo.chadwyck.com/?SOURCE=pgimages.cfg&ACTION=ByID&ID=V99567 [accessed July 2014]

Shakespeare, William, *Shakespeare: Complete Works*, ed. by W. J. Craig (Oxford: Oxford University Press, 1980).

Shelley, Mary, *Frankenstein*, ed. by Marilyn Butler (London: Pickering Women's Classics, 1993).

Shelley, Mary, *Mary Shelley: Journal*, ed. by Frederick L. Jones (Norman: University of Oklahoma Press, 1947).

Shelley, Mary, *The Letters of Mary Wollstonecraft Shelley*, ed. by Betty T. Bennett (London: The John Hopkins Press, 1980).

Shelley, Percy Bysshe, *A Philosophical View of Reform*, ed. by T. W. Rolleston (Oxford: Oxford University Press, 1920).

Southey, Robert, *The Life and Correspondence of Robert Southey*, ed. by Charles Cuthbert Southey (London: Longman, Brown, Green, and Longmans, 1849) https://lordbyron.org/contents.php?doc=RoSouth.1849.Contents [accessed July 2024]

Wordsworth, William, *The Prelude*, ed. by Ernest de Selincourt (Oxford: Oxford University Press, 1970).

Wordsworth, William, *The Prose Works of William Wordsworth*, Vol. III, ed. by W. J. B. Owen and J. W. Smyser (Oxford: Clarendon Press, 1974).

## Secondary Texts

Achinstein, Sharron, *Milton and the Revolutionary Reader* (Princeton: Princeton University Press, 1994).

Anon, 'Wordworth's Autobiographical Poem', *The Gentleman's Magazine,* 34: 188 (1850), 459–68.

Baldick, Chris, *In Frankenstein's Shadow: Myth, Monstrosity, and Nineteenth-Century Writing* (Oxford: Oxford University Press, 1987).

Baldridge, Cates, 'Antinomian Reviewers: Hogg's Critique of Romantic-Era Magazine Culture in *The Confessions of a Justified Sinner*', *Studies in the Novel*, 43: 4 (2011), 385–405.

Balfour, Ian, *The Rhetoric of Romantic Prophecy* (Stanford: Stanford University Press, 2002).

Barnard, John, *John Keats* (Cambridge: Cambridge University Press, 1987).

Bate, Jonathan, 'Keats's Two Hyperions and the Problem of Milton', in *Romantic Revisions*, ed. by Robert Brinkley and Keith Handley (Cambridge: Cambridge University Press, 1992), pp. 321–38.

Bates, Catherine, 'No Sin but Irony: Kierkegaard and Milton's Satan', *Literature & Theology*, 1 (1997), 1–26.

Bell, Vereen M., '*Wuthering Heights* and the Unforgivable Sin', *Nineteenth-Century Fiction*, 17: 2 (1962), 188–91.

Benedict, Williston R., 'A Story Replete with Horror', *The Princeton University Library Chronicle*, 44: 3 (1983), 246–51.

Bloom, Harold, *A Map of Misreading* (Oxford: Oxford University Press, 1975).

Bloom, Harold, *Poetry and Repression* (New Haven: Yale University Press, 1976).

Bloom, Harold, *The Anxiety of Influence* (Oxford: Oxford University Press, 1997).

Blumberg, Jane, *Mary Shelley's Early Novels* (London: MacMillan, 1993).

Bode, Christoph, 'Hyperion, "The Fall of Hyperion", and Keats's Poetics', *The Wordsworth Circle*, 31: 1 (2000), 31–37.

Bostetter, Edward E., 'Byron and the Politics of Paradise', *PMLA*, 75: 5 (1960), 571–76.

Boulger, James, 'Christian Skepticism in The Ancient Mariner', in *From Sensibility to Romanticism: Essays Presented to Frederick A. Pottle*, ed. by Frederick W. Hilles and Harold Bloom (Oxford: Oxford University Press, 1965), pp. 439–51.

Bronowski, J., *William Blake and the Age of Revolution* (London: Routledge, 1972).

Butler, Marilyn, *Romantics, Rebels and Reactionaries* (Oxford: Oxford University Press, 1981).

Cantor, Paul, 'Byron's *Cain*: A Romantic Version of the Fall', *The Kenyon Review*, 2: 3 (1980), 50–71.

Cantor, Paul, 'The Politics of the Epic: Wordsworth, Byron, and the Romantic Redefinition of Heroism', *The Review of Politics*, 69: 3 (2007), 375–401.

Chambers, William, *Memoir of William and Robert Chambers*, 13th Ed. (Edinburgh: W. & R. Chambers, 1884).

Chandler, James, *England in 1819* (Chicago: University of Chicago Press, 1998).

Christopher, Rovee, 'Trashing Keats', *EHL*, 75: 4 (2008), 993–1022.

Cronin, Richard, 'Keats and the Politics of Cockney Style', *Studies in English Literature, 1500–1900*, 36: 4 (1996), 785–806.

Cronin, Richard, *Romantic Victorians* (Basingstoke: Palgrave, 2002).

Cronin, Richard, *The Politics of Romantic Poetry: In Search of the Pure Commonwealth* (Basingstoke: Palgrave MacMillan, 2000).

Cross, W. L., *The Development of the English Novel* (London: MacMillan, 1899).

Dellamora, Richard, 'Earnshaw's Neighbour/ Catherine's Friend: Ethical Contingencies in *Wuthering Heights*', *EHL*, 74: 3 (2007), 535–55.

Duff, David, *Romanticism and the Uses of Genre* (Oxford: Oxford University Press, 2009).

Duncan, Ian, *Scott's Shadow* (Princeton: Princeton University Press, 2007).

Egan, Kieran, 'Relevance and the Romantic Imagination', *Canadian Journal of Education*, 16: 1 (1991), 58–71.

Eggenschweiller, David, 'Byron's *Cain* and the Antimythological Myth', in *The Plays of Lord Byron: Critical Essays*, ed. by Robert Gleckner and Bernard Beatty (Liverpool: Liverpool University Press, 1997), pp. 233–51.

Faflak, Joel and Julia M. Wright, *Nervous Reactions: Victorian Recollections of Romanticism* (Albany: State University of New York Press, 2004).

Fish, Stanley, *Surprised by Sin: The Reader in Paradise Lost* (London: Macmillan, 1967).

Fite, David, *Harold Bloom: The Rhetoric of Romantic Vision* (Amherst: Amherst University Press, 1985).

Freud, Sigmund, 'Creative Writers and Day-Dreaming', in *Poetry in Theory: An Anthology 1900–2000,* ed. by Jon Cook (Oxford: Blackwell Publishing Ltd., 2004), pp. 41–6.

Frye, Northrop, 'Blake After Two Centuries', in *English Romantic Poets: Modern Essays in Criticism*, ed. by M. H. Abrams (Oxford: Oxford University Press, 1966), pp. 55–67.

Garofalo, Daniela, 'Impossible Love and Commodity Culture in Emily Brontë's *Wuthering Heights', ELH*, 75: 4 (2008), 819–40.

Gilbert, Sandra M., and Susan Gubar, *The Madwoman in the Attic: The Woman Writer and the Nineteenth-Century Literacy Imagination* (New Haven: Yale University Press, 1984).

Grierson, Herbert, *Milton & Wordsworth: Poets and Prophets* (London: Cambridge University Press, 1937).

Hagstrum, Jean H., '"The Wrath of the Lamb": A Study of William Blake's Conversations', in *From Sensibility to Romanticism: Essays Presented to Frederick A. Pottle*, ed. by Frederick W. Hilles and Harold Bloom (Oxford: Oxford University Press, 1965), pp. 311–30.

Herman, Peter. C, *Destabilizing Milton: "Paradise Lost" and the Poetics of Incertitude* (New York: Palgrave MacMillan, 2005).

Hill-Miller, Catherine C., *My Hideous Progeny: Mary Shelley, William Godwin and the Father-Daughter Relationship* (Newark: University of Delaware Press, 1995).

Hirst, Wolf Z., 'Byron's Lapse into Orthodoxy: An Unorthodox Reading of Cain', in *The Plays of Lord Byron: Critical Essays*, ed. by Robert Gleckner and Bernard Beatty (Liverpool: Liverpool University Press, 1997), pp. 253–72.

Kermode, Frank, 'Adam Unparadised', in *The Living Milton: Essays by Various Hands*, ed. by Frank Kermode (London: Routledge, 1960), pp. 99–120.

Kitson, Peter, 'Coleridge, the French Revolution, and "The Ancient Mariner": Collective Guilt and Individual Salvation', *The Yearbook of English Studies*, 19 (1989), 197–207.

Lau, Beth, 'Romantic Ambivalence in *Frankenstein* and *The Ancient Mariner*', in *Fellow Romantics: Male and Female British Writers, 1790–1835*, ed. by Beth Lau (Milton: Routelege, 2009), pp. 71–97.

Levine, Michael, 'Pantheism', in *The Stanford Encyclopaedia of Philosophy* (Stanford University, 2012), http://plato.stanford.edu/entries/pantheism/ [accessed July 2024]

Lieb, Michael, *The Dialectics of Creation: Patterns of Birth & Regeneration in Paradise Lost* (Massachusetts: University of Massachusetts Press, 1970).

Lockhart, J. G., 'Review of *Endymion*: The Cockney School of Poetry IV', *Blackwood's Edinburgh Magazine*, 3 (1818), in *Keats's Poetry and Prose,* ed. by Jeffrey Cox (London: Norton, 2009), pp. 272–76.

Lokke, Kari, '*The Last Man*', in *The Cambridge Companion to Mary Shelley*, ed. by Esther Schor (Cambridge: Cambridge University Press, 2003), pp. 116–29.

Lovejoy, Arthur O., 'Milton and the Paradox of the Fortunate Fall', *ELH*, 4: 3 (1937), 161–79.

Mack, Douglas S., 'Hogg's Politics and the Presbyterian Tradition', in *Edinburgh Companion to James Hogg*, ed. by Ian Duncan and Douglas S. Mack (Edinburgh: Edinburgh University Press, 2012), pp. 64–72.

Madden, William A., '*Wuthering Heights*: The Binding of Passion', *Nineteenth-Century Fiction*, 27: 2 (1972), 127–54.

Mahoney, Charles, *Romantics and Renegades: The Poetics of Political Reaction* (Basingstoke: Palgrave Macmillan, 2002).

Matlak, Richard, *Wordsworth's Trauma and Poetry: 1793–1803* (Milton: Routledge, 2024).

McGillis, Roderick, 'Childhood and Growth: George MacDonald and William Wordsworth', in *Romanticism and Children's Literature in Nineteenth-Century England*, ed. by James Holt McGavran Jr. (Athens: University of Georgia Press, 2009), pp. 150–67.

McLane, Maureen M., *Balladeering, Minstrelsy, and the Making of British Romantic Poetry* (Cambridge: Cambridge University Press, 2008).

Miller, Karl, *Electric Shepherd: A Likeness of James Hogg* (London: Faber and Faber, 2003).

Miriam, Allot, ed., *The Brontës: The Critical Heritage* (London: Routledge, 1974).

Morse, David, *The Age of Virtue* (Basingstoke: Palgrave, 2000).

Newlyn, Lucy, *Paradise Lost and the Romantic Reader* (Oxford: Oxford University Press, 1993).

O'Halloran, Meiko, *James Hogg and British Romanticism: A Kaleidoscopic Art* (Basingstoke: Palgrave MacMillan, 2016).

O'Rourke, James, 'The 1831 Introduction and Revisions to "Frankenstein": Mary Shelley Dictates Her Legacy', *Studies in Romanticism*, 38: 3 (1999), 365–85.

Paulson, Ronald, 'Gothic Fiction and the French Revolution', *ELH*, 48: 3 (1981), 532–54.

Plasa, Carl, 'Revision and Repression in Keats's Hyperion: "Pure Creations of the Poet's Brain"', *Keats-Shelley Journal*, 44 (1995), 117–46.

Plotz, John, 'Hogg and the Short Story', in the *Edinburgh Companion to James Hogg*, ed. by Ian Duncan and Douglas S. Mack (Edinburgh: Edinburgh University Press, 2012), pp. 113–21.

Poole, William, *Milton and the Idea of the Fall* (Cambridge: Cambridge University Press, 2005).

Rena-Dozier Emily, 'Gothic Criticisms: *Wuthering Heights* and Nineteenth-Century Literary History', *ELH*, 77: 3 (2010), 757–75.

Richardson, Alan, 'The Politics of Childhood: Wordsworth, Blake, and the Catechism Method', *ELH*, 56: 4 (1969), 853–68.

Roe, Nicholas, *John Keats and the Culture of Dissent* (Oxford: Oxford University Press, 1997).

Roe, Nicholas, 'Revising the Revolution: History and Imagination in *The Prelude*, 1799, 1805, 1850', in *Romantic Revisions*, ed. by Robert Brinkley and Keith Handley (Cambridge: Cambridge University Press, 1992), pp. 87–102.

Roe, Nicholas, *Wordsworth and Coleridge: The Radical Years* (Oxford: Oxford University Press, 1997).

Rosenberg, John D., 'Keats and Milton: The Paradox of Rejection', *Keats-Shelley Journal*, 6 (1957), 87–95.

Schlicke, Paul, 'Hazlitt, Horne and the Spirit of the Age', *Studies in English Literature*, 45: 4 (2005), 829–51.

Schock, Peter A., 'The "Satanism" of Cain in Context: Byron's Lucifer and the War against Blasphemy', *Keats-Shelley Journal*, 44 (1995), 182–215.

Shapiro, Arnold, '*Wuthering Heights* as a Victorian Novel', *Studies in the Novel,* 1: 3 (1969), 284–96.

Simpson, Louis, *James Hogg: A Critical Study* (Edinburgh: St Martin's Press, 1962).

Sperry Jr, Stuart M., 'Keats, Milton, and the Fall of Hyperion', *PMLA*, 77: 1 (1962), 77–84.

Spiegelman, Willard, *Wordsworth's Heroes* (Berkeley: University of California Press, 1985).

Stauffer, Andrew M., Marilyn Butler, and James Chandler, *Anger, Revolution, and Romanticism* (Cambridge: Cambridge University Press, 2005).

Stone, Donald, *The Romantic Impulse in Victorian Fiction* (Massachusetts: Harvard University Press, 1980).

Taylor, Irene and Gina Luria, 'Gender and Genre: Women in British Romantic Literature', in *What Manner of Woman: Essays in English and American Life and Literature*, ed. by Marlene Springer (New York: New York University Press, 1977), pp. 98–128.

Tillyard, E. M. W., *Milton* (London: Chatto & Windus, 1966).

Tillyard, E. M. W., *Poetry and its Background* (London: Chatto & Windus, 1961).

Tucker, Herbert, *Epic: Britain's Heroic Muse 1790–1910* (Oxford: Oxford University Press, 2008).

Walker, Richard J., *Labyrinths of Deceit: Culture, Modernity and Identity in the Nineteenth Century* (Liverpool: Liverpool University Press, 2007).

## Suggested Further Reading

Brisman, Leslie, *Milton's Poetry of Choice and its Romantic Heirs* (London: Cornell University Press, 1973).

Crawford, Joseph, *Raising Milton's Ghost: John Milton and the Sublime of Terror in the Early Romantic Period* (Bloomsbury Academic, 2011).

DiSalvo, Jackie, *War of the Titans: Blake's Critique of Milton and the Politics of Religion* (Pittsburgh, PA: Pittsburgh University Press, 1983).

Fairer, David, 'Milton and the Romantics', in *John Milton: Life, Writing, Reputation,* ed. by Paul Hammond and Blair Worden (Oxford: Oxford University Press, 2010), pp. 147–65.

Fallon, Stephen M., *Milton's Peculiar Grace: Self-Representation and Authority* (Ithaca, NY: Cornell University Press, 2007).

Griffin, Dustin, *Regaining Paradise: Milton and the Eighteenth Century* (Cambridge: Cambridge University Press, 1986).

Havens, Raymond Dexter, *The Influence of Milton on English Poetry* (New York: Russell & Russell, 1961).

Hill, Christopher, *Milton and the English Revolution* (New York: Viking Press, 1978).

Jarvis, Robin, *Wordsworth, Milton and the Theory of Poetic Relations* (Basingstoke: Macmillan, 1991).

Kitson, Peter J., 'Milton: The Romantics and After', in *A New Companion to Milton*, ed. by Thomas N. Corns (Chichester: Wiley Blackwell, 2016), pp. 547–65.

Kuduk Weiner, Stephanie, *Republican Politics and English Poetry, 1789–1874* (Basingstoke: Palgrave Macmillan, 2005).

Lewis, Linda M., *The Promethean Politics of Milton, Blake, and Shelley* (Columbia: University of Missouri Press, 1992).

Schulz, Max F., *Paradise Preserved: Recreations of Eden in Eighteenth- and Nineteenth-Century England* (Cambridge: Cambridge University Press, 1985).

Shawcross, John T., *John Milton and Influence: Presence in Literature, History, and Culture* (Pittsburgh, PA: Duquesne University Press, 1991).

Teskey, Gordon, 'Milton and the Romantics', in *A Companion to Romantic Poetry*, ed. by Charles Mahoney (Chichester: Wiley & Sons, 2010), pp. 121–37.

Trott, Nicola, 'Milton and the Romantics', in *A Companion to Romanticism*, ed. by Duncan Wu (Malden, MA; Oxford: Blackwell, 1999).

# Index

For Product Safety Concerns and Information please contact our EU representative GPSR@taylorandfrancis.com
Taylor & Francis Verlag GmbH, Kaufingerstraße 24, 80331 München, Germany

www.ingramcontent.com/pod-product-compliance
Lightning Source LLC
LaVergne TN
LVHW011628120826
845149LV00022B/2671

* 9 7 8 1 0 3 2 8 6 4 3 3 4 *